"Philip Johnson's book is a valuable touchstone for anyone journeying to discover the new values that will guide us well into the next millennium."

LANCE H.K. SECRETAN,
author of *The Way of the Tiger*

"Dr. J describes the 'fix' that each of us needs — the same fix that works for economies in trouble. Take time-out and then don't just try working harder — work smarter."

PAUL F. STARITA,
Managing Partner and President,
Royal Trust Investment Services Inc.

"Thanks for the nudge. Balance is the answer. I'm going skiing."

WILLIAM ODOM,
Chairman of the Board,
Ford Motor Credit Company

"A must-read for every busy person. As I read, I kept running into myself. Philip Johnson had his finger on the pulse of my life."

ARTHUR CALIANDRO,
minister, Marble Collegiate Church,
New York City

TiME-OUT!

TIME-OUT!

Restoring Your Passion for Life, Love and Work

DR. PHILIP EARNEST JOHNSON

Stoddart

Published in 1992 by
Stoddart Publishing Co. Limited
34 Lesmill Road
Toronto, Canada
M3B 2T6

Second printing June 1992

Canadian Cataloguing in Publication Data

Johnson, Philip E., 1943-
Time Out

ISBN 0-7737-5491-1

1. Fatigue.   2. Leisure.   3. Time management.   I. Title.

BF482.J65 1992   155.9'042   C92-093291-6

Cover design: Brant Cowie/ArtPlus Limited
Author photograph: Peter Paterson
Typesetting: Tony Gordon Ltd.

Printed and bound in Canada

To Lyn

For her love,
which helps restore
my passion for
life, love and work

Contents

TIME-OUT!

INTRODUCTION

_____

"IT'S OVER."

I could hardly believe what I had just heard, two little words that ended the fulfillment of a lifelong dream. Less than two weeks before, I had begun my new job as executive director of a global leadership foundation. Now, it was over. The chairperson of the foundation did a complete reversal and pulled the plug on months of promises.

I had carefully considered the position for months. I'd flown to the site in Pennsylvania almost every week for three months to set the vision and to create a plan for its strategic success. I'd traveled across North America to confirm that the foundation was on the leading edge. My wife, Lyn, and I had held a family conference about the opportunity. Finally we'd decided to plunge boldly into our new adventure with all of its risks, both known and unknown.

It had been for me the pearl of great price. I'd closed my speaking and consulting business in Canada and made the necessary plans to take up permanent residency in the United States. We did some redecorating and put our house up for sale. We even cleaned out our basement! And Lyn and

I drove to Pennsylvania and spent a few days house-hunting. We found the perfect "house in the woods."

So much hope. So much anticipation and excitement. We had already moved there in our minds and hearts.

Then came the news. I felt like the air had been let out of my beautiful balloon. I felt disillusioned, flat, stunned. I really couldn't believe what had happened. It seemed like a bad dream that would disappear once I awoke. It didn't.

So I came back home. And did something I would never have done under these uncertain circumstances. I took time-out. Usually I would have pressed on. I would have burned up the phone lines, feverishly searching for work, never skipping a beat. I would have been extremely busy getting my vocational life on track again.

I amazed my family and friends. But mostly I amazed myself. I took a week off. A whole week! I hadn't taken that much time off in a couple of years. I relaxed. I actually played. Went to a concert. Read a novel. Spent time with our kids. And reintroduced myself to my spouse. We went dinner-dancing. And made love, several times. It was a wonderful week!

I felt refreshed and ready to get going again. I was surprised that I now had energy to sort out my predicament, pick up the pieces and put the puzzle together.

Time-out for me was a life-saver and a life-provider. I had experienced it personally and practically. So persuaded was I of its value that I resolved to write a book about what it meant to me with the hope that my experience could help others. I prepared a book proposal and submitted it to a major publisher. The rest, as they say, is history.

I knew and supported the theory and value of time-out

but somehow had neglected to fully use the tremendous scope of its renewing power. I really didn't need to be persuaded about taking it. Like many of us, what I needed was the will, the permission and the encouragement to actually take it. A reminder to take care of myself sometimes.

My hope in writing this book is that it will inspire you to call time-out to bring harmony to your life. In chapter two, I discuss its three interrelated dimensions: a principle of renewal, a discipline of growth, and a strategy of control. I'll show you how to use it effectively in the various aspects of your life.

I guarantee you won't regret it. However, I must warn you that it may overturn your life-style. It has certainly changed and enriched mine.

Each of us has time-out memories. You wouldn't be alive if you hadn't taken time-out.

Do you remember graduating and celebrating an achievement? Lying in the sun on your summer vacation? Deciding what to do after being rejected? Planning your career? Slipping into a hot soothing bath after a long demanding day? Resolving a misunderstanding with your spouse or teenager? Crawling into bed after moving day? Examining an opportunity at work? Sharing Thanksgiving dinner with your family? Taking a walk to deal with your anger?

It's not as if time-out is a brand-new concept to anyone. But if you're like me, you probably could use a little more of it more often. And perhaps use it more strategically when the need arises.

I do not profess to be an expert on the subject. I'm still learning how to use it more effectively, and I've got a long way to go. But I do want to pass on to you some of the discoveries I've made.

"What do you want in life?" This is a question usually asked in opinion surveys. The top responses are time and money, with time often outranking money!

It's no wonder.

People are like jugglers trying to keep all the balls or plates in the air — without dropping any. We are experiencing *koyaanisquatsi*, a Hopi native American word that means life out of balance — crazy life, life in turmoil, life disintegrating. Heavy responsibilities, multiple roles and ever-rising expectations exert increasing pressures on our time.

The pace of life seems too fast. In his book, *Stress and the Manager: Making It Work for You*, Karl Albrecht says, "The great defining characteristics of this period — the first three-quarters of the twentieth century — have been change, impermanence, disruption, newness and obsolescence, and a sense of acceleration in almost every perceptible aspect of North American Society."

Most of us try desperately to stay abreast of too much change, find life increasingly complex, and are bombarded with information as never before in history. A weekday edition of the *New York Times* contains more information than the average person in seventeenth-century England was likely to come across in a lifetime. We are suffering, says American architect and graphic designer Richard Saul Wurman, from "information anxiety." The amount of available information now doubles every five years.

We feel overwhelmed with too many choices — over-choice — with limitless alternatives and options. We feel powerless in determining our own future. We feel pulled in all directions.

Life seems fragmented as never before. In his *Globe and Mail* article "The Death of Leisure," Michael Posner cites communications theorist Neil Postman's belief that the two most dangerous words in the English language are the television anchorperson's "Now this." They reflect "a world of fragments, where events stand alone, stripped of any connection to the past, or to the future, or to other events. All assumptions of coherence have vanished."

But we are realizing once again that time is precious and irreplaceable. Marketing consultant Faith Popcorn writes in *The Popcorn Report: Faith Popcorn on the Future of Your Company, Your World, Your Life* that people today want to "cut back, simplify, streamline, in order to be able to live *slower* again. Achievement without exhaustion. Accomplishment with less stress. What we really want to do is to buy back time. . . . What we want now is less. More and more less."

We need to master a simple but elusive concept: taking time-out. It's the only way we'll keep our heads above water, especially during the tough economic times ahead.

Many books help readers organize their time at work and at home. There are literally thousands of books that can help you manage your time more productively and efficiently. Others seek to help men and women sort out relationships and family stresses. But what about the problem in balancing work and home, personal and community demands? *Time-Out!* is unique, because it shows readers how to bring all the disparate notes of their lives into harmony.

To present a thorough understanding of the principles and benefits of time-out, I have offered real-life practical examples of how busy men and women have effectively applied time-out in the various aspects of their lives. As well, I provide ten time-out tactics that you can use right away, practical guidelines that will help you reap the benefits of time-out. And finally, for those of you who would like to follow up a particular area of concern in greater depth, I have included a resource list.

Ultimately it is my hope that you will see how time-out prepares you for time-in — refreshed, renewed, restored and ready for life, love and work.

CHAPTER 1

The Inner Signals

ALL OF US, at one time or another, experience crises or situations that trigger feelings of self-doubt, fatigue, isolation or unhappiness. When these feelings become overwhelming, perhaps long in duration, they are inner signals warning us to step back, reevaluate, make a change, do something other than what we've been doing. These feelings may overlap, you may have had all or only some of them, but I'm sure they'll strike some chords.

Personally unfulfilled

"There's got to be more than this!"

You're trying your best and working hard, but you don't feel satisfied. Something is missing. You're not alone. Millions of people are struggling with questions about the deeper meaning of life.

You may be feeling a little discomfort. Or a lot. You may have a gentle itch that needs to be scratched. Or you may be living at the other extreme, as Thoreau described it, a life of "quiet desperation." You may be disenchanted with the world and cynical about the future because past experience tells you that things don't work out the way they're planned.

You may feel as if you're on parade, marking time, making some noise but not much progress. You may feel like the pilot who told his passengers he had some good news and some bad news. "The good news," he said, "is that we are making excellent time. The bad news is that we don't know where we're going." You may have had dreams of a brilliant future that you've had to put on hold. And you wonder if you'll ever be able to realize them.

You may feel a lack of fulfillment, especially if you have money and power. There goes the myth. Money and power do not automatically lead to fulfillment. "I possess, therefore I am," is simply not true.

"Beyond a level of comfortable survival," says Sam Keen, author of *The Passionate Life: Stages of Loving*, "goods become a substitute for the primal goodness we were denied — familiarity, intimacy, kindness."

Success may not, in fact, bring you happiness. A letter to Joyce Lain Kennedy, an advice columnist in the *Dallas Morning News*, illustrates this. "I'm forty-three, a successful professional still on my way up and unhappy. With my long hours, I sometimes feel that I'm running between the raindrops. My personal life has been a series of exploding relationships, including one divorce. I feel successful but not driving on the scenic route."

On what route are you driving? Are you getting what you want on the great freeway of life?

Many people these days are seriously seeking something to bring unity and purpose to everyday living, something that has lasting value and importance and can draw the disparate aspects of fractured lives into focus.

We long to make sense of the world and our place in it. We are desperately searching for a few moral touchstones that could provide a solid foundation for the major decisions we have to make.

We ask two basic, fundamental questions: Who am I? What is my purpose?

These questions are asked especially at what we've come to call the midlife crisis. Aptly named, it usually hits men and women in their forties. For many, it's a crisis that literally turns life upside down, particularly those who have not been relatively honest with themselves until midlife. Truthfulness with oneself is vital, especially when asking, Who am I? One thing we know for sure: how you deal with your midlife crisis will definitely affect the rest of your life.

Some of us are panic-stricken as we try to put our past, present and future in perspective. Emergency sirens sound. A keen sense of urgency takes over. What contribution have I made? What contribution could I make? Will I have time? Am I too late to make my mark in the world?

Often we see ourselves in terms of what we do for money. Our status and self-respect are relative to what we earn to spend on the things we produce. So we have to paddle faster and faster to make ends meet — or else get pulled into the depths. Lewis H. Lapham, editor-in-chief of *Harper's* magazine, in his latest book, *Money and Class in America: Notes and Observations on the Civil Religion*, says that for the majority of Americans, money is God — or at least the means to getting whatever we most desire. But, as Lapham points out, money disappoints: "Never in the history of the world have so many people been so rich; never in the history of the world have so many people felt themselves so poor."

If you were born between 1946 and 1958, you may be suffering from the "baby-boomer blues." You grew up in a promising time, a period of great expectations that continued to rise. And then, poof, the balloon bursts, and many boomers find themselves in the unenviable position of experiencing failure for the first time.

Author Amy Saltzman maintains that many baby-boomers have grown increasingly skeptical about the payoff for devoting so much time to the fast track. As their huge generation crowds toward the top of the corporate pyramid, many are getting stalled. At the same time, companies are slashing the ranks of middle managers.

Boomers are ten times more likely to be depressed than their parents and grandparents. But growing up in a time when there was a loss of belief in country, God and family, and social institutions, what did we expect? In an age that prides itself on personal control, an age of the individual, what's there to hold on to?

Overwhelmed by life's demands

Do you remember the Broadway play *Stop the World I Want to Get Off*?

A while ago I saw a woman wearing a T-shirt that said, "I've got it all: job, home, kids, guilt, stress, anxiety." I asked her how things were going and she responded angrily, "Can't you read, turkey?" Did she feel overwhelmed? You bet!

Who isn't overwhelmed from time to time? Your to-do list is endless. Everything has top priority. The sheer amount you have to deal with is mind-boggling. Twelve hundred advertising messages are beamed our way every week.

If you never feel overwhelmed, maybe it's because you're a spectator in the stands, watching life being played out before you, and not actively playing out on the field yourself.

A survey of life-styles by Priority Management Systems (Canada) Inc. shows most people working longer hours, enjoying less family and leisure time and suffering high levels of stress. The one overwhelming theme is the pressure people feel at not being able to meet the various professional and personal demands on their time.

In the survey, eighty-one percent say they suffer from stress at least once a week, and forty-eight percent report feeling stressed every day. The signs of stress, as cited by the respondents, include headaches (33.1%), stomach problems (5.9%), fatigue (7.3%), muscular tension (7.9%), frustration (20.8%) and anger (22.6%). The major causes of stress were listed as the job, interruptions, the manager or supervisor, the telephone, projects, family, the desk, peers and meetings.

One of the hazards of being fully alive is that you have to deal with a variety of life issues, some of which are very stressful. And often these issues come all at once!

Of course there are degrees of being overwhelmed. Occasionally people need to be hospitalized because the weight of their responsibilities and burdens is unbearable.

But often we are simply worn down by modern life. We face such external stresses as traffic, overcrowding, angry people, recession; maybe our private space has been invaded too.

We're "stressed out." The word "stress" comes from the Latin *strictus*, which means to be drawn tight. And tight we are. It manifests itself most commonly through headaches and anger, but also through backaches and digestive problems. The responses vary, from eating and drinking too much to yelling at children and picking fights with our spouse.

Psychologist Richard Lazarus writes: "Psychological stress resides neither in the situation nor in the person; it depends on a transaction between the two. It arises from how the person appraises an event and adapts to it. Stress is what occurs when the demands of the environment, in the person's eyes, clearly exceed the resources of the person to handle them."

My wife, Lyn, sent me an encouragement card with this inscription: "Into each life a little rain must fall . . . followed by hail and damaging winds." Sometimes life feels like that. It's just one damn thing after another. The car breaks down. There's an unexpected bill. You lose your job. There's a flood in the basement. Your child falls off her bike and you have to take her to emergency for stitches.

Overwhelmed by life's demands? Ready to throw in the towel? Don't. Listen to what your feelings are telling you: take a break.

Uncertain about the future

"The future," Casey Stengel is attributed with saying, "ain't what it used to be."

Almost everybody has feelings of apprehension about what lies ahead — for ourselves personally and for our species collectively. There are various kinds of stress: time, situational, encounter and anticipatory. The last, anticipatory stress, is the one associated with uncertainty about the future. It is expressed in degrees of concern and/or worry about what may happen in the days ahead.

Some of us have managed to frame our predicaments humorously. When asked how a person could make a small fortune today, one businessman replied, "Start with a big one!" But the truth is there's not a lot to laugh about.

We fear for our safety. We don't feel as secure as we once did. Safety and security are two of the fastest-growing industries in North America. Where is anyone safe anymore? A young man drove his pickup truck into a crowded restaurant in Killeen, Texas, and shot and killed twenty-three people, the worst mass shooting in U.S. history.

At BrainReserve, a marketing consulting firm that specializes in developing new products and services and in revitalizing existing brands for the future consumer, Faith Popcorn brought the concept of "cocooning" to our attention. She defines it as the impulse to go *inside* when it gets too tough and scary *outside*. "Cocooning," she observes, "is about insulation and avoidance, peace and protection, coziness and control — a sort of hypernesting."

People worry about their health — particularly the thirty million Americans who have no health insurance! According to a recent survey conducted by the Alliance for Aging Research, sixty-six percent of Americans hope they will live to be a hundred, despite all of the world's problems. But, the most telling statistic is that only six percent think they will make it.

For Americans older than fifty-five, the cancer mortality rate is expected to increase by as much as twenty percent by the year 2010. For those younger than fifty-five, however, the cancer mortality rate is expected to decrease by twenty-five to thirty-five percent.

The revelation that Los Angeles Lakers' superstar Magic Johnson retired from professional basketball because he contracted the Human Immuno-deficiency virus (HIV), which leads to Acquired Immune Deficiency Syndrome (AIDS), has heightened not only our awareness, but our fear of its possible ramifications.

AIDS statistics are alarming. Known cases, and deaths attributed to AIDS, increased more than five times between 1989 and 1991. The National Center for Health Statistics, in the U.S., predicts that AIDS is becoming one of the ten leading causes of death. In 1987, it was ranked fifteenth.

Perhaps the key area of uncertainty about the future concerns work. This is true especially in the light of the roller-coaster economic climate in the early eighties and again in the nineties. I asked a businessman a while ago how he was dealing with the recession. "Like a baby," he replied. "Every three hours I wake up and cry."

Many have been caught in the corporate shuffle, the new dance craze. It's a bit like musical chairs. When the music stops, there are fewer dancers.

Maybe you're one of those who is no longer dancing.

The deal used to be, not so many years ago, that a company would provide steady employment, and the employee would provide productive effort and loyalty. You were committed to the company and expected advancement. But now, thanks to slower growth and leaner and meaner organizational structures, the opportunities for advancement are limited. A more competitive marketplace, deregulation and rapid technological changes have "forced" companies to reorganize to cut costs, yet improve product quality and service.

Change, uncertainty and personnel cuts have replaced stability, predictability and growth, and management and professional ranks have been hit the hardest. There's a feeling of being unjustly treated and you also feel powerless and anxious about the future.

It's a scary world out there, and at the dawn of the twenty-first century, people are understandably uncertain about what lies ahead.

Consumed by work

From the seventies to the eighties, the average workweek for Americans increased by ten hours. And all the indications are that we're striving to set a new record in the nineties.

For many, this imbalance in life stems from an addiction to work. Not just working hard. Working hard and workaholism are not the same. Those who work hard are energized by their work, whereas workaholics crave only work, are addicted to it and are ground down by their one-dimensional existence. Working hard doesn't make you a workaholic. But being unable to stop working, or thinking about work, does.

Dr. Barbara Killinger, author of the insightful book *Work-*

aholics: The Respectable Addicts, describes a workaholic as "a person who gradually becomes emotionally crippled and addicted to control and power in a compulsive drive to gain approval and success." She describes workaholism as "a grave, cruel and dangerous affliction."

A workaholic is someone who is hooked on work. No time for play. Nose to the grindstone. One-track mind. One-track life. Life *is* work. A workaholic can be obsessive, abrasive and ruthless. The prime victims are middle-aged men. Maybe you know one. Maybe you are one.

"There is only one cure," prescribes Killinger. "Recognize your feelings in order to restore inner balance. Your values must change and you must be willing to share power and become empathetic and cooperative." Unfortunately most people who show these signs deny they have a problem, a normal symptom of addiction. So they resist treatment, many vehemently.

All work and no play makes Jack or Jill unhealthy, unproductive and dull. And in an increasing number of cases, dead! Ten percent of Japanese deaths are caused by overwork, called *karoshi*.

It is estimated that ten thousand Japanese literally work themselves to death annually, mainly managers in their forties and fifties, working more than twelve hours daily, six or seven days a week. The symptoms include dizziness, nausea, severe headaches and stomachaches. In ninety percent of the cases, death follows within twenty-four hours of experiencing the first severe symptoms.

North Americans are working long hours, too. A recent Priority Management Systems survey of business people reveals: eighty-five percent of respondents work forty-five hours a week or more; eighty-three percent work through lunch at least once a week; sixty-five percent work at least one weekend a month; and forty-seven percent spend three hours or more a week on business work at home.

In a poll conducted for *Fortune* magazine, 206 chief executive officers said that they work an average of sixty-one hours a week and expect their top executives to work an average of fifty-four hours a week.

Fifty to sixty percent of North Americans, especially men, may be described as Type A personalities, or demonstrate Type A characteristics that include: an extreme sense of urgency and impatience, unbridled anger and hostility, an all-consuming competitive drive for results, a persistent desire for recognition and advancement, preoccupation with self-imposed time restrictions and achievement of goals.

Dr. Harriet B. Braiker, an American clinical psychologist and corporate consultant, asks in her book *The Type "E" Woman: How to Overcome the Stress of Being Everything to Everybody* whether a woman can "have it all" — a career and a family. Many women, says Braiker, try valiantly to have it all by pushing themselves to "do it all" and excel. "As long as she believes that it is possible to be everything to everybody and remain untaxed or undamaged physically and/or psychologically," Braiker points out, "she is caught in a self-defeating trap. She will keep coping by trying to rise to each and every occasion, pushing herself beyond safe or reasonable limits, without adequate regeneration and rejuvenation of her resources, until she is thoroughly depleted by her own good intentions."

17

Many people today, both men and women, worship their work, work at their play and play at their worship. Their bottom line is tragic. They are living to work, rather than working to live.

Frustrated with your job

Is your job driving you crazy?

Seventy-three percent of people in a recent North American survey said they were not happy with their work. Another ten percent indicated that they were happy in their work only some of the time. There are many reasons for this unhappiness.

Some feel frustrated because of the lack of challenge. They're busy enough, but the job doesn't come close to tapping their potential. They're *bored*. And I'm not just talking about assembly-line or clerical jobs. Management positions that involve all the responsibility but no authority to call the shots aren't much fun, either. There's no room to grow or develop expertise.

Others are frustrated because they are unsuited for their present work. Round peg in a square hole. Nice shoes, wrong fit. Or the values of the individual and the company clash, and a constant unproductive battle rages. Sometimes there are ethical implications that can destroy innovative ideas. The necessity to compromise may cause incredible internal turmoil.

Still others are unhappy with their jobs because they feel unsupported. Their supervisors don't tell them what to do or how to do it. They're working in a vacuum. Management is perceived as erratic, unreasonable and unknowledgeable. In a word, incompetent.

Lack of support from superiors is observed particularly in the mixed messages that are delivered from on high: see the broad picture, and be aware of all the details too; have a healthy family life, and work evenings and weekends; take risks, but don't screw up.

A multinational vice-president believed his boss when he was told to take risks and be assured he would not be thrown under the bus if he failed. Well, he took the message to heart and took a significant risk for his company. His risk was matched with a significant failure. He was demoted immediately from his senior position, though he remained an executive. He expressed his anguish with the mixed messages he had received by attending the next executive meeting wearing a tan suit with, you guessed it, tire marks on the back and front of his jacket.

Others feel their work goes unappreciated and unrecognized. They may be bypassed for a promotion because of politics. "If you want to get ahead around here, you have to kiss ass," said one employee of a well-respected company.

I feel deep regret for women who find themselves in the "pink ghetto," with low pay and dead-end jobs. Despite a certain amount of progress, there is a long way to go before equality is achieved in the workplace.

Tired of the rat race

Have you noticed lately how most people drive on the freeways? It's as if they're driving to make this the last day of their lives!

Everybody seems to be in such a hurry. Rushing here.

Dashing there. Afraid we might miss something, we keep a frenetic pace. Studies have shown that TV viewers change stations as often as twenty-two times a minute, or once every 2.73 seconds. Media analysts describe them as "grazers." Over half of the eighteen- to thirty-four-year-olds said they regularly watched two shows at once. Twenty percent claimed to be able to follow three or more shows simultaneously!

Our pace of life as a society is accelerating at an alarming rate. A sign of the age of anxiety: a TV station in a major market announced its new program to woo time-poor viewers — "Take Thirty — an hour's news in half the time." The average length of any image seen on TV is three and a half seconds. An average of twenty-four thirty-second commercials an hour is projected at the audience. And now, with the fifteen-second commercial, we could see as many as forty-eight in an hour.

There used to be an information float, the time between a message being sent and received. But today that cushion of time has collapsed. Newspaper and magazine articles are about thirty-five percent shorter than they were ten years ago.

"It takes all the running you can do, to keep in the same place," said the Queen in *Alice in Wonderland*. "If you want to get somewhere else, you must run at least twice as fast as that!" And running twice as fast, we are.

"If there's a national plague, it's fatigue," observes trend-tracker Faith Popcorn. "We're even too tired to watch as much escapist TV as we used to."

We are a people on the run, skipping meals and eating pretzels as we sprint to our next appointment. Sales of salty snacks in the U.S. increased 5.1 percent in 1987 alone, to more than $8 billion. In 1989, we spent $900 million on microwavable foods. It is expected that the figure could reach $3 billion after 1991.

I heard a cute story about a mother going grocery shopping with her four-year-old. The child ran to her mother with a cake mix. "No, honey," she said to her daughter, "you have to cook that."

We're terrified of wasting time. We're living in the age of the nanosecond, the nine-second sound bite. Our attention span has been greatly reduced. We're captives of time.

We're tired, and it's dangerous. U.S. sleep experts estimate that sleepiness contributes to about sixty-five hundred traffic deaths and several thousand accidents a year. Entire flight crews have reportedly gone to sleep in cockpits of commercial airliners. Four Americans in ten cut back on sleep to gain more time, according to a study done by American Demographics.

We've redefined how we live by redefining time. When we're not "out of time," we have "down time," "just in time," "overtime," "travel time," "quality time" and, minimally, "quiet time." And thanks to time-saving devices, we have more time to do more!

A Hilton Hotels survey found that ninety percent of all Americans now spend nearly half of their weekend working overtime or doing chores.

Ralph Keyes, in his book *Timelock: How Life Got So Hectic and What You Can Do about It*, notes that sixty percent of the 443 subjects who filled out his questionnaire about time said that their lives had grown busier during the past year. More than half agreed with the statement "There aren't enough hours in the day to do everything I have to do." Another thirty-one percent concurred that "on the whole I have just about enough time to do what I have to do." In other words, eighty-five percent felt that they had virtually no "spare" time. As compared with ten years ago, sixty percent said they had less leisure time today.

The warning signals that you're being harmed by the rat race are there if you'll recognize them.

A man in his forties felt the telltale signals warning him to slow down. Shortness of breath. Chest pains. Irritability. Restlessness. But he pressed on anyway. Then, like a ton of bricks, it hit him. He had a heart attack late on a Friday evening at home and ended up in intensive care.

I went to see him. He told me with certainty that the attack was minor and that he would be out of hospital on Sunday. He played down his condition even though he was literally hooked up for life. He told me that he had a very important meeting to attend on Monday morning. The meeting just couldn't proceed without him. I gently tried to encourage him to postpone the meeting for a couple of weeks. But no way. I tried more forcefully. But his mind was made up and that was that.

I went to see him on Sunday afternoon. He had already signed himself out of the hospital. At his meeting the next day he made what was probably the most memorable presentation of his life. He had another coronary and died at the podium.

Winston Churchill once remarked that the "unfortunate thing in life is that we stumble over the truth, and then, get up and go on as if nothing had ever happened."

Threatened by change

Is anything new automatically suspect? Have you allowed change to take over your life rather than directing, adapting to and using it wisely?

If that's how you feel, you're not alone.

To a certain extent, we all want and need some protection from the strong winds of change that are blowing. We need to have some things that are solid, immovable, unchangeable. But very few things are today. The only constant seems to be change.

Craig Brod, a San Francisco clinical psychologist who coined the term "technostress" in his 1984 book of the same name, said that the problems caused by accelerated technological advancement are getting worse because companies aren't aware of them. He believes that the stress is from computers interacting with humans.

Brod defines technostress as "the overidentification of people to the computer . . . People get used to all the attributes of the computer: the yes-and-no answers, getting the precise answers, almost omnipresent power of data at your fingertips and work at a constant speed. People start demanding these qualities psychologically from other people . . . and this causes stress in relationships. But humans are not data dumps. They have qualities of feelings, emotions and ambiguities."

We live in a technoworld. No reason you can't be in touch instantly, anywhere. You can have constant accessibility if you choose. You can duplicate your office at home by a simple combination of a personal computer, fax, phone, modem, plus assorted software. One-quarter of American homes have cordless phones. On the road, in the air or on the sea, a laptop PC, cellular phone and portable fax will fit neatly in your briefcase. Three and a half million people have phones in their cars. On a recent visit to the zoo, I saw a man, child in one hand, mobile phone in the other, trading stocks. The orangutans pointed at him quizzically. Who's the endangered species here?

The changes taking place are pervasive and constant. Life seems an endless surprise. No wonder we feel threatened and therefore resistant to change. And yet, a no-surprises, unchanging world is impossible.

Immobilized by a crisis

You freeze. You know you need to act. Right now. But you can't. You're looking backward and forward at the same time. You're plagued by indecision. Crises have no respect for timing. They just happen. And when they do, the wind is taken out of your sails.

Marcy called her husband, Bill, at work with the news. Several years earlier she had called with similar news. Then, joyful excitement had filled her voice. Today it held a mixture of disbelief and despair. They were going to have a child — their third. Neither of them wanted another child. Their career paths were established. They had a healthy girl and boy. All was well with the world. And now this.

John was a robust man in his late thirties who loved life. Active in sports and in the community, he was happy at home, and his career as a lawyer had really taken off. Then, out of the blue, he fell violently ill and was rushed to the hospital. Tests were done but nothing particularly irregular was found. He got better and went back to work. But every once in a while, he would be overcome with dizziness and nausea. Thinking it was a bad virus, he consulted his doctor. He could hardly believe his ears when he was told that he had terminal cancer. He probably had only a few months to live.

Betty and David were having breakfast one morning before they both headed off to work. They never said much at breakfast. But this morning David was particularly quiet and pensive. Even anxious. When Betty inquired whether anything was wrong, David replied that he wanted a divorce.

Who knows what crisis you are facing or might have to face? No one is immune. And when disaster strikes, your thinking may get fuzzy, your work will probably suffer, and you'll feel drained of all energy and vitality. It's time, then, to take time-out.

Unhappy in a relationship

The divorce rate today is about fifty percent! For first marriages, it's between forty and fifty percent. Approximately seventy-five percent of divorced people remarry, half within three years. And as individuals' expectations surrounding marriage become higher, the divorce rate increases. Divorce feeds upon itself.

According to the Canadian Institute of Stress in Toronto, the corporate world offers an ideal environment for two stress-related problems: chronic fatigue and relationship breakup. Stress robs Canadian professionals of their energy and their ability to play well with others.

In 1981, American psychologists Dr. Susan Geiss and Dr. Daniel O'Leary made a survey of the problems of marriage. They questioned marital therapists and found that communication, unrealistic expectations, power struggles, role conflicts and lack of loving feelings ranked high as complaints among couples treated.

Many people, both male and female, are not only unhappy in a relationship, they feel "trapped." The person who best illustrated being trapped in a relationship was Wendy. Here's what she told me.

"We married seventeen years ago. Of those seventeen years, I think we've probably had six months of happiness, tops. We never were your happy couple. Although I had great hopes in the beginning.

"Shortly after we were married, Ken changed. He needed to control me, and for a while I went along thinking that he was going through a stage, and that after a while, it would change. Well, surprise, surprise. It never did. I guess I allowed him to walk all over me. And as I look back, we were both responsible for our state of affairs.

"Now I feel like I've been sentenced to life imprisonment. And it doesn't feel great.

"I'm angry too. I'm angry about a lot of things. But I'm really angry at the way I've allowed myself to be abused psychologically. He's never hit me, thank God. It's just a lack of order, common courtesy and consideration. I'm not asking much, just a little respect. So I suffocate here. Trapped in a relationship that's doomed."

Many who are married do not feel "trapped" like Wendy, but are unhappy in their relationship for a variety of reasons.

Out of touch with your family

Stan returned from a week-long business trip just in time for dinner with his wife and family. Their two children, aged four and seven, greeted him at the front door as if he had been away for months. They had a lot to tell him about their week. And they were eagerly anticipating going to the circus the next day.

After dinner, Stan broke the news to the kids that he had to fly out early the next morning and wouldn't be able to take them to the circus. He assured them that there would be other chances.

His four-year-old commented rather dryly, "Dad, that's what you said last time."

It's not that you purposely try to alienate your family, or leave them out or not love them. Often the pressures of work, especially if there's a lot of traveling, make it difficult to keep in touch.

Eighty percent of females and seventy percent of males say they want to spend more time with their families. The polls show that family is the most important thing in our lives, although we likely spend more time on our careers.

In a Priority Management Systems survey, fifty-two percent of respondents spend more than one hour a day with their children and spouse, and sixty-five percent spend at least one hour a day with their spouse. Twenty-seven percent spend less than fifteen minutes a day playing with their children, fifty-three percent spend less than two hours a week looking after their children, and forty-two percent report not spending any time reading to their children.

Several years ago I attended a course where one of the leaders, a psychiatrist, asked us to make a list of our priorities. Quickly I put down "family" at the top of the list. Then he invited us to put the number of hours we devoted weekly to each of our priorities. The result was devastating. My family, which I claimed to be my top priority, was given nowhere near the appropriate time.

There are two symptoms to watch for that will give you a clue that you're out of touch with your family.

First, you can't communicate with them. Family life is based on good communication, and when the lines are cut off, you can't grow as a family. One evening I got a call from the police. A young boy had been picked up for shoplifting, and his father, when contacted, refused to go get his son. So I went and took the boy home. I had a chat with his father, who said that his fourteen-year-old son was a jerk. I replied that he may be acting like a jerk, but underneath he was a good kid. I asked when he had last talked with his son. He said he couldn't remember.

The second symptom is an inability to get along. There is constant friction, arguing and disharmony. As a family you may have a major attitude problem. There's no sense of caring for one another's welfare, and it shows.

A lack of trust is usually at the root of family discord. Somewhere along the line the bond of trust, if established in the first place, has been severed. And with the demise of trust goes respect. Nothing can be dealt with, or any behavior contained, when there is no trust or respect. Where a family lacks these two ingredients, the members are decidedly out of touch.

A sad but true story may give you the nudge you need to take time-out if you're out of touch with your family. A thirteen-year-old boy committed suicide by hanging himself from a tree in his backyard. He left a note on the kitchen table. "Dear Mom and Dad. I had to do this. This was the only thing around here with roots. Love."

Have you experienced any of these inner signals? I'm sure you have. When you're feeling personally unfulfilled, or consumed by your work, or tired of the rat race or unhappy in a relationship, maybe it's time to take a break. Maybe it's time for time-out.

CHAPTER 2

What Is Time-Out?

WE ALL KNOW that time-out is a break. A period, long or short, when you withdraw, voluntarily or involuntarily, from your usual activities. I have divided time-out into three related dimensions: a principle of renewal, a discipline of growth and a strategy of control.

Principle of renewal

Time-out is a principle based on a fundamental assumption about life: human energy can be renewed.

Work is absolutely essential. But so is rest, rejuvenation and recreation, which derives from the Latin verb *recare*, meaning to recreate, renew, replenish.

It's a natural rhythm, one built into our psyches. Getting in synch with it helps us find real meaning in life. We are created to use the energy we are given at birth. The creation story describes our energy as the breath of life. It's a free gift to be used, not stored. If we use energy, we can take time-out to allow this energy to be restored. It's an awesome principle. Amazing when you think about it. And so simple.

Chapter one is about the inner signals that alert you to your need for time-out. They're like a fuel-gauge light blinking, letting you know you're low on fuel. It's time to fill up.

You don't have to worry about a shortage of fuel. There's no limit. And the price is right. The deal is that if you take time-out, you'll receive the energy you need to be radically alive. I had that experience when I took a day to play in the Grand Canyon in Arizona. What a tremendous feeling of exhilaration. I felt at one with the earth and all of nature, with myself and others.

"We have little control over eighty-five percent of the things that happen to us each day," suggests psychologist James Paupst. "The only control we do have is how we let them affect us." That point of view is affirmed by psychiatrist Abraham Maslow, who once observed, "You are the product of what you choose for your life situation. You do have the capacity to make healthy choices for yourself by changing your attitude to one of creative aliveness."

Dr. Bernie Siegel, a general surgeon for thirty years and for many years an assistant professor of surgery at Yale University Medical School, recalls a cancer patient once telling him that it was all right for her to come to the doctor, but how was she supposed to live between visits? Seigel was stunned by what the patient had to go through emotionally day by day. He now travels around the world presenting workshops, talks and seminars to people with serious illnesses, as well as to people in the health-care field. His therapeutic approach integrates body, mind and spirit as he explores the role of hope, love, spirituality and unconscious beliefs in the healing process.

"It's what we do with adversity that makes the difference," he says. "Some people need a death sentence proclaimed before they let go of all their restraints and start to really live."

I believe the work/rest model is similar to the recurring life-cycle. We are born. We live. And we die. We are given energy. We expend it by living fully. New energy is born in us. And so on.

We are also given time, the gift that is linked to our energy and its renewal. We have to devote time to reenergize ourselves, or we will wither and eventually die. Taking time-out enables us to be whole human beings, to fulfill our potential, to revitalize our entire selves. Our high calling is to give ourselves away so that we can be reenergized to give ourselves away again. Over and over and over again. It's a wonderful economy of love and growth and maturity.

The time-out principle of renewal is universal. It applies to everyone at every age and stage of life. The infant needs time-out as much as the eighty-five-year-old. It also applies to all situations. Commitment of time for the purpose of time-out is essential in all the dimensions of your personal, intimate and family life, as well as your workplace and career.

Discipline of growth

Several years ago, *Guidepost* magazine printed a letter from an older man who reflected on his life and expressed his regret. "If I had my life to live over," he wrote, "I would relax more. I wouldn't take so many things as seriously. I would take more chances. I would climb more mountains and swim more rivers. I'd ride more merry-go-rounds. I'd pick more daisies."

Time-out gives you the opportunity, and the responsibility, to discipline yourself, so that the principle of renewal is activated.

The discipline is very simple. You use energy. Then you decide to take time-out to renew your energy. You're the one who has to discipline yourself. The discipline is rooted in a belief in yourself.

Trust the feelings that signal the need for time-out. We are very creative at covering up our feelings. From time to time, we deny them altogether, usually to our regret. But don't — your natural rhythm is alerting you to the need to take a breather.

The discipline of time-out is something of a paradox. You take time-out to benefit time-in. Time-out is not an end in itself. The primary object of taking time-out in the game of life is to renew you, so that you can get back in the game to give your best. A military unit retreats — takes time-out — in order to advance. In an intimate relationship, the players may choose to be apart for a while so that they can be truly *present* for each other upon their return.

To some degree, and perhaps this is the most difficult aspect of time-out to come to grips with, you must give yourself permission to surrender time, to take time-out, so you can strive again with renewed energy.

We should also discipline ourselves to take *regular* time-out, for our overall health and well-being. Take regular breaks from the rigorous intensity of life and work, regular time-outs with your family and friends. Annual checkups, reports and meetings reflect this discipline. The great thing about making time-out a habit is that you are better prepared to take a spontaneous or emergency time-out.

Disciplining ourselves to take regular time-out is a preventative measure. Resistance to disease and disappointment is increased. People who take time-out regularly simply don't get sick as much or as often, and they are more resilient in times of adversity.

I remember my grandfather Johnson teaching me a valuable lesson about this. He was a remarkable carpenter. After dinner, when we visited, he would invite me to come down to his basement workshop to sharpen the saws, a nightly ritual. He sharpened and set each tooth of his seven saws with great care. When he was finished, he'd place the saws in his toolbox as if they were precious instruments, all ready for the next day's work. Then he'd turn, look me straight in the eye and say, "Now, Philip Earnest (Earnest was his name too), let's sharpen you." Then he'd ask me questions about almost everything.

Time-out is about being on the cutting edge, about ensuring that we are ready for the tasks ahead, about renewing our energy so we can be all we were created to be.

The consequences of not taking time-out range from mild discomfort to death. If you don't take time-out voluntarily, you may suffer burnout, a significant term that indicates that you're running on empty. The discipline of time-out keeps an eye on the gauge and never waits for your energy supply to reach dangerously low levels. This is done almost unconsciously.

A heart attack is a dramatic signal. Don't be like the man who refused to heed it, went on to his business meeting and died at the podium. A heart attack should force time-out. It's nature's way of reminding you that you need to review how you're living and probably make some adjustments, including a new appreciation for and practice of time-out.

Time-out is a discipline that will enable you to thrive as an individual. It will help you to become the person you were created to be. It will stretch your capacity to grow and mature physically, mentally, spiritually and socially. Although these four aspects are interconnected, I shall talk about them separately, because renewal of any one of them is beneficial for holistic growth.

Time-out for physical development is perhaps the best place to start, even if it's just regular exercise and healthy nutrition. Physical growth has immediate measurable benefits.

About five years ago, I got some pretty clear signals about my physical state. Actually, loud sirens with bright pulsating lights! I caught a bad flu virus. I decided right there and then that I had to get into shape, take responsibility for my physical well-being and follow a routine that would build up my strength, flexibility and endurance. I'd made that promise before. But this time I followed through. And I've never felt better. Honest.

It wasn't a picnic at first. Time-out can be painful and you must not be fooled into thinking it's not. It can reveal a truth you don't particularly want to know, accept or deal with.

I didn't really want to know the results of my first

complete medical and fitness test. It indicated that I was performing at the level of a sixty-eight-year-old! Not great news for a supposedly active guy in his early forties.

But eventually it was worth the pain to know and act on reality. I haven't had as much as a cold since. My counselor at the fitness club where I was a member prepared a personalized program that helped me improve gradually until I reached a maintenance level. I now work out for about an hour and a half at least four times a week to keep in shape, and also to train for hurdling, a sport in which I was very active in high school. In August 1989, I competed in the World Masters Games Track and Field Championships in Eugene, Oregon, and in my age category(forty-five to fifty), made it to the final in the 110-meter hurdles.

We have a vast capacity to develop mentally, but research indicates that most of us use less than ten percent. What a waste!

Opportunities for continuing your formal or informal education for life are available in every imaginable area of interest. It takes discipline to think, or read, or write, or plan. And with the knowledge explosion, it's difficult to know where to begin. But you were meant to use your mind throughout your life. I've noticed that people who discipline themselves to grow mentally, generally ask more questions than those who do not.

A few years ago, I had the pleasure of visiting a parishioner who was in her late eighties. She had a long history of community involvement and was still a driving force in the Women's Institute, in Canada. She was bright and customarily read three or more newspapers every day, always including the *New York Times*. She claimed that keeping mentally alert was one of the keys to her longevity.

Then there's spiritual growth. This is about taking care of your soul. It's the discipline that helps you identify your basic beliefs and shape your values. It gives your life a "why" and energizes you from the inside.

The form of time-out you take to renew yourself spiritually varies widely according to your assumptions about your being. My assumption is that God is love and that my spiritual time-out to make a daily connection with the Creator renews my strength. Meditation, prayer and worship with others are meaningful ways for me and many others. Perhaps the biggest challenge in this area is just being still. Holding on to our lives so tightly, many of us are reluctant to loosen our grip and let go. Find the ways that are most appropriate to you to help you grow spiritually.

Social growth is a discipline that requires incredible energy. It's not just coping or surviving, but achieving peace with yourself and with others. Feeling like a worthy human being, connected to the people around you.

Life is a cooperative venture. You are given the opportunity to form relationships that help you to be emotionally unified, as well as help others to fulfill their potential. Cultivating relationships by taking time-out just to be with family and friends renews our courage, because we know we can count on these people who share our dreams and take them as seriously as we do. Taking time-out with your family, usually the most supportive of all those around you, is particularly vital.

A man confided to me that his deepest regret was not

having spent time with his children during their formative years. He explained that he had been preoccupied with his work in that period and rarely saw his spouse or family. And when he did, there was no real communication. He didn't intend to hurt them. And now, he didn't know how to relate to his teenage son, who was heavily into drugs.

Take responsiblity for your development as the unique human being you were created to be. Believe in yourself. Take time-out to grow physically, mentally, spiritually and socially.

Strategy of control

Time-out is a dynamic strategy of control that has four key elements: timing, pacing, centering and focusing. Learning to recognize and integrate these elements helps us take control of our personal and professional lives more effectively.

TIMING

"Time-out!"

Basketball coaches are very skilled at calling time-out. They have an incredibly keen sense of timing. They instinctively know when a time-out will give their team a competitive advantage. Whether their intent is to preserve a lead when the opposition is having a hot streak, or to regroup the team to improve its performance, strategic time-out can and does play a major role in the outcome of the majority of games. I saw a game where time-out was called with less than four seconds left to play. Then in one seemingly continuous motion, the ball was thrown down the court to a forward, who in turn took a jump shot that hit the mark and proved to be the decisive basket of the game.

In life, as in basketball, although there does not have to be opposition, the timing of the call is critical, some would say everything. Anticipating what may happen if the current situation continues, and determining the best time to call time-out, is largely intuitive and improves with experience. There is no perfect time to call time-out. Some times are just more or less advantageous than others. The key is to be able to call time-out before a situation deteriorates or becomes impossible to turn around. Occasionally we are faced with events that have already occurred, and we call time-out to deal with them.

On October 18, 1989, I was leading a seminar on coaching for about a hundred sales managers with a major brokerage house. The participants all wore hats with their company logo and the word "coach" in corporate colors. Each also had a whistle.

Early that afternoon, the senior vice-president entered the seminar room with a rare degree of urgency, blew his whistle and called time-out. The group thought that it was a part of the seminar, but soon realized that this was a real time-out. As you may recall, that was the day the stock market took a severe nosedive. Their coach acted very strategically by calling time-out. By the way, I took no credit for what was a memorable learning experience. Timing is absolutely critical.

PACING

When your human engine is racing, it's next to impossible to think clearly. Slowing down the pace by calling time-out enables you to deal with life's challenges carefully and creatively. Time-out is like a Slow, Curve sign, warning you to slow down so you can deal with what's happening now and what's on the road ahead.

If you're constantly living in the express lane, maybe you need to take time-out and transfer into the collector lanes. Or maybe even make a pit stop.

A family argument that's approaching the boiling point needs time-out to cool down before irreparable damage occurs. In the international arena, we witnessed prior to the January 15, 1991, deadline set by the United Nations for Saddam Hussein to leave Kuwait, a fervent call for time-out. Hundreds of thousands worldwide demonstrated for peace, requesting that cooler heads and hearts prevail among the leaders so that a disastrous war could be averted.

CENTERING

When you slow the action of your life, you are then able to look inward calmly and call upon your inner resources — your personal center of power. The most important thing in life is not what *happens* to you but what you *do* with what happens to you. So, tapping into your personal center of power — centering — is an essential aspect of taking control of your life. Time-out provides the context for centering.

A mother of four children ranging in age from four to

sixteen was exhausted from the heavy demands placed upon her. Meals to prepare. Housekeeping. Driving the children to and from school and lessons. Managing all the schedules and so on and so on. Further, one of their children is physically disabled and requires constant attention. Fortunately her husband was sensitive to her needs. One Friday night, he surprised her with a weekend getaway at a spa. He took care of everything, allowing her a very welcome time-out. She had a couple of days to do whatever she wanted, when she wanted. She had a fabulous time. She was able to find and draw upon her inner strength, and she returned to her family refreshed.

FOCUSING

Abraham Lincoln once remarked, "If we could first know where we were, and whither we are tending, we could better judge what to do, and how to do it."

This is focusing. Time-out provides the environment to find your center and then focus this inner strength on the future, direct the flow of energy toward your objective. Your objective may be to celebrate your success, educate yourself, resolve a misunderstanding in an intimate relationship, explore the possibility of changing jobs or just veg out. Time-out focuses the energy of your life to accomplish your goal. It's a time to stand back from the trees to see the forest, to focus on those things that are really important to you and plan to realize them.

For more than five years I have been conducting a Time-Out program for senior corporate leaders. The program encourages time-out from their busy schedules once a month for half a day, to reflect and focus. Let me assure you that's a major commitment of time for a president or a chief executive officer. Although they find it difficult initially to spring themselves loose from a pattern of rarely slowing down, let alone stopping, they discover that time-out is an invaluable tool not only to center themselves and regain personal strength and courage, but to focus their attention on the critical concerns only they can address.

Time-out ends with a whistle for time-in. The action begins again. Part of the focusing process must include a plan for reentry, just as NASA plots the reentry of its spacecraft. The real success of any time-out can be judged on what effectively happens when you return to the game.

Time-out is a principle of renewal, a discipline of growth, and a strategy of control. It can change your life and influence positively those around you. It will energize you if you discipline yourself to take it. And it can give you the context for strategic success. All contribute to the natural flow of life. As it says in Ecclesiastes, "For everything there is a season, and a time for every matter under heaven: a time to be born, and a time to die; a time to plant, and a time to pluck up what is planted."

One of the best ways to learn how to use time-out in your own life is to see how other people have used it effectively. The next six chapters provide examples of real people who have taken time-out for their personal, married, family, work, vocational and community lives. In some cases, details have been changed to protect the identity of persons written about.

Time-out worked for these people. It can work for you.

CHAPTER 3

What Time-Out Can Do for You

IN RESEARCHING THIS BOOK, I asked people, like you, what they wanted most in life. Their responses formed the basis of this chapter on what time-out can do for you. Although not a panacea, time-out helps you get what you want in life — meaning and purpose and perspective. It can restore your passion for life, love and work, so you can reduce stress, do what you love, risk with resilience, experience intimacy and foster family life.

Discover purpose

Shakespeare's Hamlet states, "This above all: to thine own self be true/And it must follow, as the night the day/Thou canst not then be false to any man."

In the summer of 1987, Robert Perkins, at the age of thirty-seven, left his job on Wall Street as an insurance executive in search of his true self. He flew to Yellowknife to spend some time alone in the Arctic wilderness.

For seventy-two days he paddled on the Back River through six hundred miles of ice and tundra to become the first solitary canoeist ever to reach the river's mouth at the Arctic Ocean.

He also discovered himself, the purpose of his quest. When he returned to "civilization" he made a quietly dramatic film, entitled *Into the Great Solitude*, that captures the spirit of his quest to find the primary person in his life: himself. The title of the film derives from an Inuit shaman who once said that "true wisdom is always to be found far away from people, out in the great solitude. Solitude and suffering open the human mind, therefore a shaman must seek his wisdom there."

Well, you say, you'd like to find yourself but haven't got the time or the resources to make a solitary journey like Perkins. But you don't necessarily have to travel anywhere to discover your purpose in life. Time-out anywhere will help you discover who you are, find your center, the source of all meaning. Because the real secret of who you are is not in the wilderness but is right inside you. Shirley MacLaine wrote about the journey to her center in her bestselling book *Going Within*.

Erich Fromm, in *To Have or to Be*, suggests two modes of existence struggling for the spirit of humankind: the *having* mode, which concentrates on material possession, acquisitiveness, power and aggression, and is the basis of such universal evils as greed, envy and violence; and the *being* mode, which is based on love, in the pleasure of sharing, and meaningful and productive rather than wasteful activity. Most of the time it's a matter of striking a purposeful balance between the two.

"People are not giving up on material goods, but there's more letting go of the need to acquire," comments psychoanalyst Douglas LaBier about contemporary society. "The desire to have, to get, to possess becomes more in balance with other aspects of life."

"Tie your self-esteem too narrowly to your paycheck and you'll be in trouble," says Laurence Shames, author of the book *The Hunger for More: Searching for Values in an Age of Greed*.

Psychotherapist Steven Berglas sees a growing realization that the eighties' symbols of success — a prestigious and time-consuming job, a six-figure salary and an abundance of material possessions — are incomplete. "People are saying, 'I've got money and I've got power, but it's worthless unless I can be happy.'"

Daniel Yankelovich, a world-renowned social analyst, agrees. He hypothesizes that, among Americans, there is a "shift from pride in having to pride in doing" and suggests that the "materialistic free-for-all" of the eighties has come to an end. A February 1989 survey by the Gallup Organization was entitled "Public Values Intangible Assets More than Material Possessions."

The truth is you have everything you need to become everything you want to become. It's all within you. Your potential is waiting to be realized, and time-out can assist you in finding out what really makes you tick. What makes you happy. How you survive and what hurts you. For Perry, a New York street person in the movie *The Fisher King*, there are three things in this world that you need: respect for all kinds of life, a nice bowel movement on a regular basis and a blue blazer. What do you need? What makes you happy? Take time-out to find out.

Gain perspective

Orson Welles was once reminded by his doctor to keep perspective. Orson was advised to give up those little intimate dinners for four, unless there were three other people eating with him. In the award-winning movie *Hoosiers*, a small-town basketball team from Hickory, Indiana, reaches the state final to everyone's amazement, including the players themselves. Their coach, realizing that getting to this level was a quantum leap for his players, takes them to the giant stadium where they are scheduled to play. They're in shock at the size of the place. The seats seem to go up for miles. The coach asks one of the players to measure the distance from the floor to the rim of the basket. It is, of course, the same as at home. The team's perspective is brought into focus.

The word "perspective" comes from the Latin *perspicere*, which means "to see through." Having perspective is the capacity to see the relative importance of people, places and events, to see the whole picture and be able to sort things out and set priorities now while keeping the past and future in mind.

You've got to keep your focus in life to maintain perspective. If you don't have a clear sense of where you're headed, it's next to impossible to keep perspective. It's so easy to lose.

We all need perspective because, as psychiatrist M. Scott Peck began his book *The Road Less Traveled*, "Life is difficult.

This is a great truth, one of the greatest truths. It is a great truth because once we truly see this truth, we transcend it. Once we truly know that life is difficult — once we truly understand and accept it — then life is no longer difficult. Because once it is accepted, the fact that life is difficult no longer matters."

So we have to live one day at a time. People try to live otherwise, but it's not possible. Unless you're Muhammad Ali, who puts a different twist on perspective: "Age is a matter of mind over matter. If you don't mind, it don't matter."

Reduce stress

Want to reduce your level of stress? Who doesn't!

Some stress is necessary for you to live. "Complete freedom from stress," said Hans Selye, "is death." But too much stress can lead to burn-out.

From time to time, you need to reduce the pressures of everyday living so you can think and feel and act in a more relaxed way. Time-out helps you reduce stress effectively by enabling you to control the pace of your life.

Most of the time it's a matter of slowing the action, maybe even stopping the action once in a while.

I enjoy watching golfers who are able to slow their thoughts and ultimately their swing to get maximum distance and accuracy in their drives off the tee. I once saw Jack Nicklaus at the Canadian Open. His movements between shots are much faster than those of most players, and sometimes appear to be pressured. But at address, his move-

47

ments become slow, deliberate, calculated. Once the powerful swing is over, he quickly resumes his normal tempo.

You can slow the action of your life by taking time-out. You'll feel more relaxed and attain a sense of calm. You'll see things more clearly. You'll lighten up, not take life so seriously, and smile, laugh and play. Play is an important part of life in general and time-out in particular. So is physical exercise, whether it's a brisk ten-minute walk or two hours of pumping iron. A great form of time-out to reduce stress.

You'll also be able to reduce stress by diffusing, or at least containing, such difficult situations as family arguments. When the stress level is high, things are said and actions taken that are destructive and might not have been said or done at all if the stress level had been reduced.

The latest craze in reducing stress by time-out are what have been dubbed "power vacations" or "breakations." These are mini-vacations of two or three days. Evidence is that more people are taking shorter, more frequent holidays instead of the two- or three-week vacation. A recent travel-industry survey indicates that about seventy percent of all pleasure trips now last three days or less.

A word of caution about breakations comes from Dr. Lucille Peszat, Director of the Canadian Center for Stress and Well-Being: it takes twenty-four to forty-eight hours to truly unwind. The brain processes more than fifty thousand pieces of information a second, and so you can see you have a complex mechanism to slow down.

It's a matter of personal preference how you reduce stress with time-out. Some are turned on by a week of skiing or sailing; others by various New Age retreats for the burned-out, which offer austere accommodation, vegetarian meals and concentrate on meditation and yoga. I talked to a New Yorker who told me that when he gets wound up tighter than a drum, he jumps into his truck and heads upstate. "There's something about being up there," he said. "I come back feeling like a new man." I feel that way, too, when I spend an hour or two hiking in southern Ontario's Elora Gorge or sit on the point at our cottage.

And when I can't get away to one of my favorite restorative spots, I simply close my eyes and take mental mini-vacations that produce feelings of serenity, calm, and peacefulness. Time-out will reduce stress and help you get in touch with your real feelings. Then you can be true to yourself.

Do what you love

- An advertising executive leaves his job, gets a degree in counseling and now works with a family-services center.
- A medical doctor gives up his practice to do what he has always dreamed of doing, driving a bus.
- A multinational vice-president resigns and finds his enjoyment teaching kindergarten.
- A Roman Catholic priest now heads up a company that makes diagnostic kits for diabetics.
- A high-school teacher leaves the teaching profession and starts his own small business.
- A forty-six-year-old construction company president and owner sells his profitable business and enters nursing.

The above are people who took time-out and are now doing what they love. You, too, can do what you love. And love what you do. Studies show that your job is second only to your age as the most important predictor of health and behavior.

In a 1991 survey of 2,400 Canadian workers by the Wyatt Company, seventy-five percent said that what they *do* is important for their happiness. Workers want job satisfaction. In a recent national U.S. survey of corporate personnel officers, workers now rate job satisfaction as more important than job security, and "more money" came in third.

The reason most people don't have work that is satisfying is that they have never taken the time to articulate their purpose. And if you don't know where you're headed and why, you only live from moment to moment, aimlessly, with minimal satisfaction.

But if you want to explore who you are and what is unique about you, then the possibility of doing what you love is closer than you think. The American mythologist Joseph Campbell talked about following your bliss. Your passion. And when you follow your bliss, Campbell claimed, doors will open for you that you didn't even know existed. I believe that. I'm living proof that when you do what you love, miraculous things happen.

What are you good at? What gives you the most pleasure? What would you like to do more than anything else in the whole world? The choice is yours.

There may be lots of obstacles to overcome. Demosthenes wanted to become an orator. But he had a major problem: he had a speech impediment. And yet, so persuaded was he that he could follow his bliss, he spent countless hours on the seashore filling his mouth with pebbles to overcome the impediment. And overcome it he did. In the end, he became the world's most famous orator.

Time-out can help you pursue your calling, what you were called to do. To pursue your mission in life. Viennese psychiatrist Victor Frankl maintained that you detect rather than invent your mission in life. "Everyone," he said, "has his own specific vocation in life . . . therein he cannot be replaced, nor can his life be repeated."

When you do what you love, it shows. I had a math teacher in high school who truly enjoyed his calling. He could make the numbers come alive and equations a thing of beauty. I learned a lot about math and a lot about life from him. A Toronto-based radio broadcaster, Peter Gzowski, also exemplifies doing what you love and loving what you do. His tone of voice says it all. No matter whether he's interviewing a world leader or a farmer from the Maritimes, Peter has the capacity to bring out the best in people.

Time-out helps you do what you love. Sometimes it may mean changing jobs. For many that's what happens. For others, it can affirm and breathe new life into what they're doing now. Either way, you win!

Keep your balance

It is increasingly important for people to establish balance in their lives. Balance of the whole person is the number-one health issue of the nineties, and the key to survival into the twenty-first century.

Studies done at Michigan's Survey Research Center have found that subjects expressing frustration with their lives come disproportionately from two groups: the ones who always feel rushed, and those who have time on their hands. It's a third, middle group — those who sometimes feel rushed and sometimes have time to spare — who are most likely to be satisfied with their lives overall.

I'm talking about personal balance, but also the balance between ourselves and technology. As John Naisbitt said in *Megatrends*, "Technology and human potential are the two great challenges and adventures facing humankind today. The great lesson we must learn from the principle of high tech/high touch is a modern version of the ancient Greek ideal — balance . . . We must learn to balance the material wonders of technology with the spiritual demands of our nature."

Fostering a healthy integration and balance among life's four basic dimensions — physical, mental, spiritual and social — is at the very heart of your well-being. It's helpful for me to frame this balance concept in the shape of a cross with spiritual at the center, balancing the personal and financial on one axis and professional and physical on the other.

In a Time/CNN poll of five hundred adults, sixty-nine percent said they would like to "slow down and live a more relaxed life," compared with only nineteen percent who said they would like to "live a more exciting, faster-paced life." A majority of those polled, sixty-one percent, agreed that "earning a living today requires so much effort that it's difficult to find time to enjoy life." When asked about their priorities, eighty-nine percent said it was more important these days to spend time with their families, and fifty-six percent felt strongly about finding time for personal interests and hobbies.

The Roper Organization, a company that conducts polls, recently published a telling statistic in the October 1991 issue of *Goodlife* magazine. For the first time, the share of adults who said that leisure is more important to them than work (forty-one percent) was greater than the share of those who thought work was more important (thirty-six percent).

McGill University professor Witold Rybczynski in his book, *Waiting for the Weekend*, shows how reserving leisure days at regular intervals is a custom of almost all societies. He cites G.K. Chesterton's three-fold description of leisure: as being allowed to do something, as being allowed to do anything and as being allowed to do nothing. Rybczynski contends that we are losing the freedom to do the last — nothing.

Fortune magazine has been interviewing twenty-five-year-olds periodically for the past thirty-five years and has found that these young workers have changed from being quietly confident of a secure future in the 1950s to being impatient, arrogant and materialistic in the 1980s. The most recent group, interviewed in 1990, have different attitudes from those of their predecessors: leisure, family and life-style pursuits are as important to this group as work.

The balance between work and family is crucial to your well-being. A recent study showed that ten percent of respondents left a job because of family and work conflicts. Organizations are aware of this conflict and are initiating more family-friendly workplace policies, including compressed workweeks, flexible hours, parental leaves, emergency leaves, elder-care information networks, day-care information networks, workplace day-care centers and job sharing. The benefit to the organization is an increased ability to attract and retain good employees, lower absenteeism and improved employee attitudes.

In our family we have a set of Christmas chimes. It's an inspiring traditional celebration of light and movement when all the candles are lit and the chimes begin to sound. To me it symbolizes the delicate balance we must strike among all the dimensions of our lives. If any one weight is missing, it throws the whole action of the chimes out of balance. So it is with life.

Embrace change

Heraclitus said that "you cannot step twice into the same river, for other waters are continually flowing in."

Time-out helps you embrace change in order to accept it, anticipate it and manage it. Accepting change, making it an ally or a trusted friend, requires that you let go of yesterday. That doesn't mean you throw out the baby with the bathwater. Or that the past is unimportant in the greater scheme of things.

On the contrary, your past is the foundation on which you create and build your future. Yes, you create your future. You invent it. Too many people are content merely to respond to change rather than seeing themselves as a creator, an agent of change. We all have in us the power to change ourselves and the world. This power is the foundation for the hope of the world.

A fundamental belief in our individual selves makes embracing change possible. American psychologist William James wrote: "Man alone is the architect of his destiny. The greatest revolution in our generation is that human beings, by changing the inner attitudes of their minds, can change the outer aspects of their lives."

Change is inevitable and always involves loss. That means that with every change there is an alteration to the status quo that can be threatening and/or releasing. The real trick in embracing change is to retain a sense of who you are and what you value. If these remain strongly held, letting go of yesterday won't be nearly as painful and will lead you to embrace change fully.

Time-out helps you embrace change by anticipating it. You'll look forward to tomorrow, anticipating the possibilities and the hurdles you have to overcome. Alvin Toffler, futurist, makes this point clearly in his new book, *Powershift*; anticipating the future will be the key, not only to staying alive on this planet, but for humanity to grow to its full potential.

If we want to make it together as a society on planet Earth, we'll have to catch the natural rhythm of life and train ourselves to see around corners, to see what's likely to happen up ahead. Kristin Shannon, who chairs Pacific Rim Research in Sausalito, California, does just this. She trains senior executive leaders to use the intuitive side of their brain to see what's coming down the pike. The skill she teaches is called "remote viewing."

Take time-out to embrace change. The benefits of embracing change include gaining a sense of control over your life, calming your anxiety and giving you a rare intuitive stability.

Make a fresh start

Have you ever gotten into a project or a business venture or a relationship and felt the urge to go back to square one? Or been forced by circumstances outside your control to start over?

In 1887, fire destroyed Thomas Edison's entire laboratory. Ongoing experiments and plans for many inventions were completely lost. To make matters worse, Edison had no insurance to cover the loss of the building. As he watched the fire smolder, he said, "We start building tomorrow."

On September 11, 1984, an out-of-control car swerved in front of singer Barbara Mandrell's silver Jaguar, and the two vehicles crashed head-on. The other driver was killed instantly. Barbara suffered a number of near-crippling injuries, including a shattered right leg and a severe concussion. She spent twelve days in a Tennessee hospital's intensive-care unit. She withdrew and wanted only to be left alone. She was able to marshal her spiritual, physical and emotional reserves and got her life back together. A year and a half after her accident she made a fresh start. She walked onto the stage and sang "I thank the good Lord I've got you in times like these" to the welcome cheers of friends and fans.

Elizabeth Taylor. Oops! There's a woman who's hooked on fresh starts. Now fifty-nine, she recently married Larry Fortensky, thirty-nine, whom she met at the Betty Ford Center in Rancho Mirage, California, in 1988.

There's a wonderful story, the truth of which I have not been able to confirm, about a San Antonio baseball team. Apparently, one season the team got off to a bad start. Great hitters but nobody was connecting. The team manager had this crazy idea. One day he brought a wheelbarrow into the clubhouse. He asked the players to throw their bats into the wheelbarrow. Then he took the bats down the street to be blessed by a self-proclaimed faith healer. The manager returned, bats blessed, and gave the good news to his players. The next day, they began to hit and went on to win their division title that year.

There is such a thing as "second wind." It's a physiological event that often follows the heavy demands placed on the body's metabolism in the first minutes of exercise. Once the adjustment takes place, heart, lung and blood functions are adequately serving the heightened demands of exercise, and the initial labored breathing stops.

Beginnings demand endings. You've got to let go of the past, bring closure to loss and sometimes dissolve relationships. Too often people try to make a fresh start without dealing first with their past, and they live to regret it.

A wonderful feeling comes with starting fresh, of giving birth to a new dream, of starting with a clean slate, a *tabula rasa*. It's wonderful because it's the result of commitment. Johann Wolfgang von Goethe, the nineteenth-century German poet, novelist and philosopher wrote:

Until one is committed, there is hesitancy, a chance to draw back, always ineffectiveness. Concerning all acts of initiation and creation, there is one elementary truth the ignorance of which kills countless ideas and splendid plans; that the moment one definitely commits oneself, then Providence moves too. All sorts of things occur to help one that would never otherwise have occurred. A whole stream of events issues from the decision, raising in one's favor all manner of unforeseen incidents and meetings and material assistance that no man could have come his way. Boldness has genius, power and magic in it. Begin it now.

Time-out helps you put the "genius, power and magic" in your beginning. Time-out helps you make a fresh start.

Risk with resilience

An older respected friend of mine told me not to follow where the path may lead, but to go instead where there is no path and leave a trail.

The chief mark of a pathfinder is a willingness to risk. So says Gail Sheehy in her book *Pathfinders: Overcoming the Crises of Adult Life and Finding Your Own Path to Well-Being.* And my hunch is that many of you reading this book recognize that in life, if you want to move ahead, you've got to risk. Maybe not hugely. But risk nonetheless.

Risk is relative. Risk to one may not seem risk to another. I talked with a man who belonged to a parachute club that met on weekends for the thrill of free-falling and drifting to earth. I commented to him that parachuting was quite dangerous. To which he replied, "I'd jump out of a plane any day before I'd argue with my wife."

There are some people, maybe you're one, who could be described as stress-seekers. They look for and enjoy activities that heighten their adrenaline levels. "We're like teabags," suggests Bruce Laingen, former hostage in Iran. "We don't know our own strength until we get into hot water."

Whatever kind of risk you take, it means that you have to loosen your grip on the sure and certain, the safe and secure. "It must be considered that there is nothing more difficult to carry out," wrote Niccolo Machiavelli, "nor more doubtful of success, nor more dangerous to handle, than to initiate a new order of things."

It's mostly fear that holds us back from risking. It holds us back from personal and professional development. Nothing is one hundred percent sure. Except maybe death and taxes.

Time-out can help you effectively deal with your fear. It can help you assess the risk you're contemplating. People who run or shoot rapids routinely assess or judge the danger level of a stretch of river. Emerson said that "knowledge is the antidote to fear." Taking the time to carefully assess the risk builds confidence, because you'll have an appreciation from your present vantage point of what lies ahead.

You'll also learn from failure, probably the most significant form of learning. At the H.J. Heinz Company, the tradition is to celebrate an "excellent" failure by shooting off a cannon.

Failure is an indication that you are growing. If you're not failing, maybe you're not stretching yourself as a person. Writer Arthur Gordon was once advised by Thomas Watson, Sr., the founder of IBM, to double his failure rate. As a writer, I have learned to live with failure in the form of rejection.

Wherever the opportunity arises, you'll increase your chances of risking with resilience if you celebrate and build on your success. You don't have to climb Mount Everest to celebrate your successful risk-taking. Little risks can give you the confidence to take bigger risks that may dramatically alter your life. Celebrate who you are, your accomplishments, your skills. All risk-takers I know don't hesitate to celebrate.

Risk with resilience. "Let us so live that when we come to die," said Mark Twain, "even the undertaker will be sorry."

Experience intimacy

Closeness. Communicating without speaking. Just knowing. Shared hopes and dreams. What is intimacy for you? How would you define it? More important, how does it feel? Because intimacy is more experienced than defined. Our capacity for and experience of intimacy is part of our human nature.

When I'm asked by a young person "How will I know I'm in love?", I respond with a seemingly superficial and facile answer: "You'll know." But it's true. Intimacy is a deep relationship between human beings that connects soul to soul, mind to mind, heart to heart, and when you have it, you *know*. Time-out is a key way to nurture intimacy. I know of no other means to so effectively nourish a relationship.

I have been most fortunate in my life to have had intimacy that has inspired and sustained me. Lyn, my wife of twenty-two years, is my lover, the mother of our two children and my best friend. She has taught me much about intimacy, especially since intimacy was not really one of my family's strengths.

How do I describe our intimacy? The best way is as a dance. Lyn has a dance background. Our daughter, Jill, is a professional ballet dancer. And I tap-dance a little and enjoy it. There is an ebb and flow to our relationship that is similar to the movement of the dance. I was delighted to read Harriet Goldhor Lerner's book *The Dance of Intimacy*, in which she articulates a good deal of my persuasion about intimacy.

"Real closeness occurs most reliably," she comments, "not when it is pursued or demanded in a relationship, but when both individuals work consistently on their own selves. By 'working on the self' I do not mean that we should maintain a single-minded focus on self-actualization, self-enhancement, or career advancement. Working on the self includes clarifying beliefs, values and life goals, staying responsibly connected to persons on one's own family tree, defining the 'I' in key relationships, and addressing important emotional issues as they arise."

Experiencing intimacy enables us to grow as individuals and helps others grow, as well. Intimacy is truly a mutual affair. There is an appreciation we develop for one another that helps us to be uniquely ourselves. There are no perfect intimates. A man was searching for the perfect wife. One day he discovered her. He was ecstatic and he asked her to marry him. She refused, saying that she was looking for the perfect husband.

61

It's a well-known fact that loneliness is bad for your health. Sharing life deeply with other people increases your immunity and your resistance to infection. You have a longer life expectancy. Reaching out and touching someone is a healing act in itself. Physical touching is necessary for health and human development. Someone studied hugs and projected that we need four hugs a day for survival, eight for maintenance and twelve for growth.

Time-out helps you experience intimacy by providing the opportunity to share. To share each other's presence, dreams and support. It also provides one of the best venues for great sex. Time-out sex seems to have a romantic quality of its own. But bear in mind that sex does not equate real intimacy. I remember a woman saying to me in counseling that she and her husband made love regularly. But it didn't make her feel close to him. What she really yearned for was for them to hold hands and have a conversation.

In the seventies and eighties, many left their marriages to "find themselves." In the nineties, by contrast, people will probably stay in their married relationships to "find themselves," to grow and change together. In other words, perhaps love in the nineties will not be blind. Susan Hayward, who conducts the Yankelovich Monitor, a study of American values, reports that the nineties will see "a social revolution as big as the one that took place in the sixties. We've given up our focus on the rights of the self, and we've decided that connection with other people is a tremendously important part of what we want out of life."

I hope you have family and friends with whom you can take time-out to experience intimacy. One of the joys of life is the knowledge that you're not alone. That others consciously, actively, form a support network for you. They believe in your dreams as much as you do.

Time-out helps you keep your commitment to those with whom you are intimate, to mature in love individually and collectively, and to face the struggles and experience the joys together. To love, experience intimacy, is hard work. Sometimes painful. But it can be incredibly satisfying.

Foster family life

A Decima poll, commissioned by *Macleans* magazine, found that seventy-seven percent of the respondents said family life is the most important aspect of their lives.

And royalty concurs. Despite rumors of marital discord, the Prince and Princess of Wales, on their October 1991 visit to Ontario, requested that there be no engagements on their daily schedule before ten-thirty in the morning, so they could spend time with their two sons, nine-year-old Prince William and seven-year-old Prince Harry.

Time-out helps families grow together, allowing each member to develop to his or her full potential. Families provide a solid base for freedom and responsibility. They hold up the promise of caring, of giving and receiving, making us feel we belong.

Family time has become increasingly important for me and our family. Just doing things together and just being together is essential to our well-being. Others are making a similar discovery.

Peter Lynch, a forty-seven-year-old investment superstar,

who masterminded the building of the Fidelity Magellan into a $13 billion mutual fund, rejected the rat race to spend more time with his youngest daughter, almost seven. He felt he hardly knew her. So in the spring of 1990, he quit work, stunning Wall Street. Sure, he had a comfortable nest egg estimated at $50 million, but many ordinary people evidently felt a connection with what he did, for he received more than a thousand letters of support. "I loved what I was doing," he confided, "but came to a conclusion, and so did some others: What in the hell are we doing this for? I don't know anyone who wished on his deathbed that he had spent more time at the office."

Time-out fosters family life in three ways. First, it builds family tradition. Every family has a certain way of doing things. Families, like individuals, have patterns that are developed over the years that distinguish them from other families. Some families cultivate these traditions more than others.

One of the traditions in our family was that we got to open one present on Christmas Eve. It was our choice. As kids, we would look over the loot and select one. There was great anticipation over the choice and the discovery of the package contents. We have passed that tradition on to our kids, and they will probably pass it on to theirs.

Not too long ago, the mother of a rebellious sixteen-year-old told me a story. Her son complained bitterly about the way his Christmas stocking was hung. "Here's this kid with a Mohawk haircut, dressed in clothes from another era, whose compliance with family rules is negligible, giving me you-know-what because his stocking wasn't hung as it usually was." We all need traditions. Rich traditions authenticate that home can be where the heart is.

Second, time-out fosters family life by making memories. Lots of memories to help us recall our life together. Memory is a stabilizing force. Memories of Thanksgiving dinner. Of weddings. Of funerals. Of picnics in the park. Of vacations. Of family rebellions — and reunions. Of religious celebrations. Of births. Of a child's first steps.

The family photo album is still a great source of remembering the memories created by family time-outs. Every once in a while, on a Sunday afternoon, my family will stroll down memory lane with ours. I'm always struck by the evolution of hair and clothing styles. And the laughter that generally accompanies the pictures.

I suggest to families that they keep a family memory jar so they can capture those time-outs together for future reference. It works. Every time you have an experience, put a note in the jar describing it. It's the stuff family biographies are made of.

And third, time-out reinforces and interprets family values. Family life is often difficult and stormy. Time-out can provide the safety for persons to work out their differences without causing the breakdown of the family. Time-out encourages an environment of trust and respect that leads to harmony.

So. What are you waiting for? Time-out can enhance every area of your life. You can't lose, and you can't afford not to take it.

CHAPTER 4

Time-Out
for Your
Personal Life

WHEN I LOOK BACK on my life, one event, more than any other, grabbed my attention, shocked me into awareness. It was the sight of my nine-year-old daughter, Jill, standing at the side of my hospital bed in intensive care, her young face filled with worry.

It was just after noon on October 16, 1979, the day I passed my doctoral oral exam. I'd had an esophageal attack, similar to a heart attack. I had heard the beep, beep, beep of the heart monitor hundreds of times before. But this time it was different. This time it was sounding out the beat of my own heart.

Suddenly I realized I had to take time-out. For my daughter and son, my wife, my friends. For *me*.

Running on empty

The warning light had been flashing for a long time. But I

ignored it. I was on a *mission*, for God's sake, and didn't have time to slow down. In fact, it hurt to slow down. It was excruciatingly painful. So I kept on. Sixty-five- to seventy-five-hour weeks were the rule, not the exception. Hooked on work. Every bit as addicted to work as some are to alcohol. I defined myself by my work. That's who I was.

I was suffering from burnout, described by psychologist Samuel H. Klarreich in his book *The Stress Solution: A Rational Approach to Increasing Corporate and Personal Effectiveness*. "Burnout," he writes, "is the depletion of your resources, both physical and psychological, caused by a compulsive desire to achieve, due to exaggerated expectations which you feel must be fulfilled and which are typically, but not always, job related. Once these are not fulfilled, there is an overwhelming tendency towards cynicism, pessimism and negativity."

I'd always felt that I had to do everything perfectly. Since childhood, that was the way I had learned to live. The real danger in trying to complete every task to perfection is that the question is always, "Is this good enough?" And the answer is, unfortunately, no. I was afraid to slow down. Afraid of boredom. Afraid of discovering the real me.

Dave Jackson, a Toronto-based industrial psychologist and chair of People Tech Consulting Inc., says that "workaholic executives often set personal standards that are impossible to achieve, living in mortal terror of disappointing an imagined, nonexistent judge." So I worked incredibly hard, ceaselessly, driven to please.

Signs and symptoms of burnout may include the following: fatigue, depression, moodiness, loss of appetite, insomnia, feelings of anger, isolation from colleagues, friends and family, behaving irresponsibly or lackadaisically, feeling strong urges to do something extreme and unconventional.

My esophageal attack was one of the best things that ever happened to me. It forced me to take time-out and set me on a new path. I once read this invitation to live: If I am not for myself, who will be for me? If I am not for others, who am I? If not now, when?

For many, like me, there is never enough time. A survey for Hilton Hotels concluded that even when people acknowledge having more free time, they report a time crunch — the feeling that they have not used their time productively, that there is no time for fun. Almost forty percent say they cut back on sleep to make more time. And nearly half those polled said they'd be willing to trade a day's pay for an extra day of free time.

Many people work long hours primarily because of fear — fear of inadequacy, fear of intimacy, fear of failure — and sometimes because they simply don't know how to use free time constructively.

It seems that where we live is important to our attitude toward time. We know there are Type A people. But are there Type A cities? California State University psychologist Robert V. Levine and his colleagues examined the "pace of life" in thirty-six U.S. cities, nine in each of the four regions. They noted the following: how fast folks walked along a main downtown street on a clear summer day; how long bank clerks took to change two twenty-dollar bills; how long postal clerks took to explain the differences between regular, certified and insured mail; and what proportion of men and women observed in the downtown area during business hours were wearing wristwatches. The results were reported in an article in the 1990 September-October issue of *American Scientist*. People in the Northeast walk faster, make change faster and are more likely to wear a watch than people in other parts of the country. New York City did not head the list of fast-paced cities. Boston headed the list, followed by Buffalo, then New York. The slowest urban pace was on the West Coast, as might be expected, with Los Angeles taking slowest-city honors.

You don't have to wind up in intensive care to be persuaded to take time-out. The food isn't great, anyway. And the lights are on all the time. But you can cultivate the time-out habit. It's your call. And there's an urgency about it. Because life's too short!

Consider taking the tombstone test. It's an effective way to help you get a handle on where you want to go and why. Just think about what you'd like to have inscribed on your tombstone when you die. It's a very revealing exercise. What legacy will you have left? What contribution will you have made to your family, your country, your world? What few words will describe the effect your life has had on others?

Alfred Nobel took the tombstone test, and it completely changed the direction of his life. One morning in 1888, Nobel, the inventor of dynamite who had spent his whole life amassing a fortune from the manufacture and sale of weapons of destruction, awoke to read his own obituary in the newspaper.

The obituary was a result of a simple journalistic error. Alfred's brother had died in the night, and a cub reporter carelessly reported the death of the wrong brother. Anyone would have been disturbed under the circumstances, but

Alfred Nobel was horrified. He saw himself as the world saw him: the dynamite king! As far as the general public was concerned, this was the entire purpose of his life. None of his true intentions — to break down the barriers that separated people — were recognized or even given serious consideration. He was quite simply a merchant of death. For that alone he would be remembered.

Nobel resolved to make clear to the world the true meaning and purpose of his life. In his last will and testament, he expressed his life's true ideals. The result was the most valued of prizes given to those who have done most for the cause of world peace: the Nobel Prize.

Dr. Hans Selye, to whom we owe much of our contemporary understanding of stress, offers these practical guidelines for handling stress that could lead to burnout: practice self-awareness and be honest with yourself about your personal needs, preferences, abilities and weaknesses; keep an optimistic attitude, putting negative beliefs into perspective and gearing energy to finding positive solutions; make personal choices that are in your best interest; and learn to use your stress-energy, because there is a limited supply.

I have learned to keep an eye on my personal energy gauge. When I see the needle moving toward empty, I know what I have to do.

I'm not creative

About halfway to Toronto on a flight from Chicago, I said to the woman next to me, "Tell me, 24A, how are you enjoying your book?"

"Fine, 24B," she replied. "It's about education. I'm a kindergarten teacher. By the way, my name is Betty."

We talked for a while about the marvelous opportunity she had to use her creativity with her children in the classroom. "But I'm not creative," she said.

"Why do you say that?" I asked.

"I've never been," she replied. "I wish I were, but I'm not."

As we chatted, it became clear to me that, from early on in her life, the message had been indelibly inscribed inside her: "Betty is not creative." Her father and one of her teachers contributed especially to persuade her that indeed she was not creative. Betty believed them. Her lack of faith in herself and in her capabilities fulfilled the assessment of others.

Even though she was not thought by some to be creative, Betty was also expected to perform at her best in everything — I mean everything! — she attempted.

Feeling compelled always to do your "personal best" is appropriate for the Olympics. But we need to learn the necessity and pleasure of doing things in an "average" way. There are some things not worth doing well. The constant pursuit of excellence can often lead to the stress of success.

I told Betty that I believe everybody is creative, and that everybody has their own unique way of expressing their qualities, attributes and gifts. She protested vigorously.

I reached into my briefcase and took out one of my business cards. On it I wrote, "Dear Betty, This is to certify that you are creative. Love, Philip." I handed her the card. She accepted graciously.

71

What I did was to call time-out for Betty. Occasionally we can do that for each other to help each other grow and think of ourselves in positive ways, ways that are not destructive. When we arrived in Toronto, she thanked me again for the card and we said goodbye.

Going through customs and immigration at Pearson International Airport in Toronto, she was asked for her ID. Then the agent asked her if she had anything to declare. "Yes," she said confidently. She paused, then said, "Yes, I'm creative."

"Pardon?" asked the agent.

"It's a long story," she replied.

I smiled. Betty smiled. So did the agent. "I'm really happy for you," he muttered.

About six months later I received a letter, a sentence. "Dear Dr. J. Thanks! Love, Betty." There was no return address on the correspondence. Wherever you are, Betty, you're still creative!

Out of synch

"Happy birthday to you. Happy birthday to you. Happy birthday, dear Keith. Happy birthday to you." The words rang hollow for Keith. He smiled appreciatively and gave all the signs of being thrilled with their efforts to celebrate his fortieth birthday. He had hoped there wouldn't be anything. But friends will be friends. So here they were together celebrating Keith's being over the hill.

His physical age was not what really got to him. He knew he wasn't twenty-five — his image in the mirror told him that. No, the problem was more than skin deep. It went to the heart of his being.

Life didn't seem to hold any purpose for him anymore. There was no meaning. No joy. He felt lonely, even among his friends at the party. He was out of touch with his feelings. He didn't even know what emotional needs he needed filled. And he got no satisfaction from his job as an engineer.

His wife put on a wonderful front at the party, but anyone with half an ounce of sensitivity would have guessed that this was not a happy couple. Their marriage was in trouble.

Keith was showing signs of being in a midlife crisis. He felt out of synch with himself and his family and his job. Guy Corneau, a Canadian psychologist, who conducts weekend retreats in which men learn to broach the barriers that separate them, says in his book *Absent Fathers, Lost Sons*, "Many men feel dead in the body, empty between the head and the groin." This described Keith.

He called a personal time-out. His response, because he had the resources, was to take a leave of absence from his job and embark on a quest to find himself. He began asking questions that seekers ask. Who am I? What contribution have I made? What contribution do I want to make? Is it too late?

He took the quest very seriously, perhaps too seriously. Maybe he should have taken the advice of the playwright George Bernard Shaw: "Every busy man should go to bed for a year when he is forty."

Keith spent some valuable time away by himself, spent time with his family and sought professional help to help him get a handle on his past, work through his difficulties and gain perspective.

He returned to his job about six months later with a sense of purpose to his life, a renewed professional direction and a feeling of being in synch with his inner self. The one learning that has affected him profoundly is his realization that life is not a destination but a journey. And his marriage? Well, they're still working on that.

In *To Catch an Angel, Adventures in the World I Cannot See*, by Robert Russell, there is a description that I see as an apt metaphor for keeping in synch. The author, who is visually handicapped, describes how he arranged things in his family cottage on the St. Lawrence River so that he could go fishing all by himself:

> So that I can go out by myself whenever I please, I have run a wire down to the end of the dock, where I have mounted a large electric bell. Before I go down to the dock, I plug the line into an outlet in the house. A timing device permits the bell to ring only once every thirty seconds. If I row too far upwind to be able to hear the bell, I can still fish without anxiety because I can always drift downwind and then I am again in touch with my base. And a man needs a base to quest from, and he needs the sense, that however far he has strayed, return is still possible. Confidence that he has such a base is all that gives him the courage to reach past the edges of the familiar. The river lies before me, a constant invitation, a constant challenge, and my bell is the thread of sound along which I return. To a quiet base.

Angry as hell

Ever been angry? I mean really angry? Flames shooting out of nostrils. Smoke rising from your ears. Muscles tight. Blood pressure off the scale.

We all know how the climate of life today sets us up for anger: choking traffic, overcrowding, excessive noise, recession-related anxieties, discrimination, unacceptably restrictive rules and regulations.

When you're feeling angry, give it a break.

The person who illustrates this best is Carl. I met him the day of his twenty-two-year-old son's funeral. I didn't know the family, but was asked at the last minute if I could conduct the service.

It's easy to understand why Carl was so angry. His only son — he had two daughters also — had been killed needlessly in a motorcycle accident. He had been a passenger on a motorcycle recklessly driven by a relative.

Just two weeks before, his son had married. So much love and hope and promise. But now, there was no hope, no promise, and love was left asking why. Carl was devastated. And angry. Angry as hell.

Carl came to my office door and stood in the doorway. "I can't do it. I can't do it. I'm so angry I can't go into the sanctuary for my son's funeral." I listened until his rage subsided somewhat, and then asked him if he would consider a suggestion. I told him it was okay for him to feel angry and that it was essential he attend his son's funeral. Since his anger was preventing him from doing so, I asked him to call time-out, to give me his anger for safekeeping

75

until the service at the cemetery was completed. Then I would give him back his anger. He agreed.

Many believe that repressing anger is extremely unhealthy. "Anger is a killer," Dr. Leonne Valois told a conference on holistic medicine recently in Winnipeg, Manitoba. If anger isn't emotionally expressed it often manifests itself in sleeplessness and heart attacks. "Any psychological problem that has not been dealt with has got to go somewhere and they go to the body."

By contrast, Carol Tavris, a Los Angeles psychologist, says that recent research all points to one finding: showing anger nearly always makes you angrier. In her book, *Anger: The Misunderstood Emotion*, she dispels the myth that you'll feel better if you let all your anger out. She says that studies show that "sometimes the best thing you can do about anger is nothing at all. Let it go, and half the time it will turn out to be unimportant."

Carl did attend the funeral. He wept. He mourned the death of his son. He celebrated his son's life and his continuing memory. And as soon as I had uttered the final words of blessing at the grave, Carl looked at me and I gave him back his anger.

Time-out can effectively give you the space you need to deal with your anger, or other strong feelings you may have.

Psychologist Dr. Richard Earle, president of the Canadian Institute of Stress, an organization that teaches stress management, says, "A lot of people today are walking around in a red-hot emotional state, one degree below boiling. It takes only the slightest provocation to make them boil over."

A motorist, already late for work, sat fuming in his car

when the morning rush-hour traffic came to a standstill. He found that he could beat the traffic by driving illegally on the gravel shoulder. But here, too, he met frustration, when he came up behind a car parked on the shoulder. Furious, he leapt from his vehicle, shouting and cursing, and attacked the parked motorist with a baseball bat.

Psychologist Dr. Christopher Webster heads up the Impulsivity Research program at the Clarke Institute of Psychiatry in Toronto; the program seeks to understand why the most insignificant incident can trigger such a massive response. In many cases, the behavior results because of negative early conditioning. "In childhood," says Dr. Webster, "they learned by observation that the appropriate way to respond to frustration was to blow your top and hurl abuse."

Such people are unaware of the inner dynamics that lead to the explosion, says Dr. Nathan Pollock, a Clarke Institute forensic psychologist. He adds that it is essential for them to become familiar with the symptoms of the mounting anger — the hot face, the clenched fists, the tense muscles, the pounding head, the tightness in the chest. Deep-breathing techniques are very helpful, and so is positive self-talk, when you describe to yourself, in positive terms, the incident that provoked you.

When did you last laugh?

Sometimes the trigger for time-out is as simple as reading a line from a magazine article. It's as if the words leap off the page and take front and center stage of your attention.

This happened to Sharon as she read about Norman Cousins's heroic battles to cure his illness with laughter. Norman wrote a book called *The Anatomy of an Illness*, which documents how he cured himself by watching hours of humorous movies that caused him to laugh and heal himself.

Sharon's eyes came back again and again to the title of the article: "When did you last laugh?" She couldn't remember. That prompted her to call time-out, to take an inventory of her life.

Dr. William Fry, a Stanford Medical School psychiatrist, reports that with laughter your lungs, heart, back and torso get a quick workout, and your arm and leg muscles are stimulated. After a good laugh, your blood pressure, heart rate and muscle tension subside, leaving you relaxed.

Sharon used to be a happy person, but lately it seemed she didn't have much to laugh about. Her marriage was in the doldrums. Her husband of twelve years showed emotion rarely, except his hostility, and feared any kind of real intimacy.

Her two daughters were a saving grace; she at least found some joy with them. But Sharon realized that she was generally very tense. She didn't exactly know how she'd come to this point in her life, but at age thirty-seven, she felt as if she were living proof of Woody Allen's comment that some people feel miserable and other people feel horrible. Sharon felt both.

She decided to search for what could help her laugh again, as well as fill the deep void in her soul. I suppose you could say she was having a faith crisis. She identified that throughout her life one of the things that gave her perspective and

78

a sense of worth was her faith in God. She hadn't thought about her faith in a long time.

So she searched everywhere for the magic that would turn her life around. She read books. Tried meditation. Took yoga classes. Looking for that single solution. Maybe I should go back to church, she thought. It probably wouldn't hurt.

That's how I met Sharon. She said to me later that I must have known she was coming that Sunday because I preached a sermon entitled "The Secret Is Inside You." The lights went on. Bells rang. And she began to laugh again. Gradually.

Her renewed commitment to God resulted in a happier life. And to her surprise, her husband asked if she would mind if he came to church with her. Now their weekly time-out helps them bond as a family. And keeps them laughing.

In his article "Many Therapists Now View Religious Belief as Aid, Not Illusion," in the September 10, 1991, *New York Times*, Daniel Goleman notes that a growing number of psychologists are finding religion, if not in their own lives, at least as an important influence in many of their patients'.

Dr. Allen Bergin, a psychologist at Brigham Young University, in the lead article in the January 1991 *American Psychologist*, argued that "there is a spiritual dimension of human experience which the field of psychology cannot ignore. Some ways of being religious correlate with greater mental disturbance, while others correlate with greater levels of mental health." His research shows that it does not matter so much the particular creed people hold, but rather how they hold it.

A *Homemaker's* magazine poll released in October 1991

showed that two out of three believe that religion plays a "somewhat important" or "very important" role in their family lives.

Not all personal time-outs result in discovery. It often takes a long time for things to work out. But you've got to start somewhere.

Burning the candle at both ends

He felt the pain in his chest right after he climbed aboard an Amtrak train traveling to New York City from Bethesda, Maryland. He knew the symptoms, and when he got off the train in New York, he went straight to the hospital. He had suffered a mild heart attack and was confined to hospital for two weeks and another four out of the office at home.

It is estimated that fifty percent of all health-related problems can be attributed in one form or another to stress. People with few social or economic resources have triple the heart disease death rate of those with money or someone to confide in, a new study shows. "If you are a patient with heart disease and you have neither love nor money, your prognosis is worse," says Dr. Redford Williams of Duke University. Williams says people who were not married and had no one to talk to had three times the disease death rate of people who were not socially isolated.

In early October 1989, Bill Marriott, president of a company that is one of the largest employers in the U.S., had a heart attack. The message of his forced time-out was clear: adjust to a slower pace. Find some balance.

A devout Mormon, no alcohol or tobacco, he adjusted

his hectic work schedule, which had previously left little time for relaxation and none for exercise. "You just can't keep burning the candle at both ends or there won't *be* any candle," he said. "I've decided to make more time for my family and more time for myself. I'll still be working hard, but I'll make more time to smell the roses."

And smelling the roses he is. He has carved out more time to spend with his family, including his four children and nine grandchildren. He has reduced his outside activities but is still active as president of the Washington, D.C. stake — a group of eight to ten congregations of the Mormon Church — and serves on the boards of General Motors, the National Geographic Society and Boy Scouts of America.

Instead of visits to two hundred of his 534 hotels, he will visit only a hundred. No rich desserts. Fourteen-hour work-days have been reduced to ten or twelve, and he has cut his travel. He has also adopted an exercise regimen and has supervised workouts on a treadmill and a bicycle.

"It is clear that moderate levels of fitness offer consider-able health benefits," claims Dr. Steven Blair of the Aerobics Institute in Dallas, Texas. "The key is moving from the unfit category, thirty to forty million in the U.S., to the moder-ately fit category. By beginning programs of moderate, regular exercise, half an hour each day, three times a week, anyone can join this group, and markedly lower their death rates from all-cause mortality, cancer and cardiovascular disease."

The Association of Quality Clubs and the President's Council on Physical Fitness and Sports declared the benefits of exercise in these findings: physically fit men are fifty-three percent, and fit women ninety-eight percent, less at risk of premature death than sedentary men and women; fit men die four times less often, and fit women sixteen times less often from cancer than unfit people; fit women have a fifty percent lower rate of breast cancer than sedentary women; fit people are eight times less likely to die from cardiovascular disease than unfit persons.

The association also claims that regular exercise reduces illness, blood pressure, stress, insomnia and the risk of diabetes and osteoporosis, as well as helps keep an optimal body weight and composition. Exercise helps the mind overcome depression, and increases creativity and reasoning power. It enhances sexual performance, weight loss and can increase the resolve to quit smoking. Older exercisers boost their intelligence because of generally improved circulation, particularly to the brain; a fit seventy-year-old has the same oxygen-carrying capacity as an unfit person of thirty. With convincing evidence like that, you may want to have a stretch break right now!

Taking time-out for your personal life is the foundation on which all other time-outs are built. You have to know yourself before you can be true to yourself. And it's especially hard to get things together in a world that seems to be falling apart. Fortunately, time-out helps us to heed the Algerian proverb that says, "Live as if you were to live forever; live as if you were to die tomorrow."

CHAPTER 5

Time-Out for Your Marriage

THE ANCIENT PHILOSOPHER Empedocles, living on the southern coast of Sicily about 440 B.C., asserted that two grand forces rule the universe. One is love, the other strife. Love unites all things. Strife separates.

Erich Fromm once said that humankind's most basic fear is a dread of being separated from other humans.

No sparking zone

Helen sat in the easy chair in my office and unfolded the story of her nineteen-year marriage to Ed.

They had a romantic beginning with a chance meeting in England. It was love at first sight. They were married six weeks later and continued to enjoy traveling together and pursuing their careers. Both were successful in their endeavors. Although they had at one time contemplated having children — Helen had contemplated it more than Ed — they did not have any.

"Intimacy" derives from the latin *intimare*, which means "to announce" or "to make known," and *intimus*, which means "innermost." You have true intimacy when you make your innermost self known to another and allow another to make him or herself known to you.

Intimacy is a matter of trust. It's not only something you do; it is a way of being that finds expression in your daily living. The human foundation of intimacy is friendship. You can't force intimacy. Barriers to intimacy include unreasonable expectations, fear of loss, holding on to the past, resentments, trying to change others and needing to be needed.

When Helen described the sexual dimension of her marriage, she kidded, "At our house there ought to be a sign that says, Welcome to the No Sparking Zone." According to Helen, their lovemaking early in their relationship was quite spectacular. She didn't share the details, but there was a glint in her eyes when she told me.

But now it was different. "If you were going to make a movie about our love life," she said, "you'd have to call it On Frozen Pond." And then she looked out the window and began to cry. "No sex for nine years." She repeated that phrase — first with no feeling, then with anger, then with sadness and finally with resignation.

Most men and women rank companionship above sex as a reason to marry. And when the honeymoon's over there are inevitable barriers to sex. Researcher Dr. Constance Avery-Clark at the Masters & Johnson Institute in St. Louis, documented that career-oriented women had more trouble getting in the mood for sex than those who are unemployed or in boring jobs. The factor of limited time for intimacy accounts for the difference. "These couples," she says, "are often unable to spend much time together because of their demanding schedules, and the career wives frequently report difficulty making an effective mental transition from their professional lives to personal time with their respective husbands."

Helen couldn't remember what had triggered her and Ed's drifting apart from each other, but over the years, they had moved from a queen-size bed to separate beds, then to separate rooms. Not only did they not have sex, they merely coexisted with minimal communication or interaction; no good kitchen-table talk, which often leads to better bed talk. They didn't even get angry with one another. The flame of love had flickered and died long ago, and their relationship was pitch-dark.

Marriage is an unusual gamble — most times, you both win or you both lose. Dr. Harville Hendrix, author of *Getting the Love You Want: A Guide for Couples*, writes, "Divorce merely eliminates the person and keeps the problem." Only five percent of all couples, he suggests, resolve the power struggle and go on to create a deeply satisfying relationship. Apparently the trouble starts when "the pleasing inviting dance of courtship draws to a close, and lovers . . . now have to satisfy a whole hierarchy of expectations, and some concerns, but most hidden from their awareness."

"Divorce," says Dr. Constance Ahrons, associate director of the Marriage and Family Therapy Program at the University of California in Los Angeles, "can cause more stress than the death of a spouse."

Helen called time-out to address her situation. She mustered the courage to talk frankly with Ed. The biggest and often toughest job is recognizing there's a problem. Ed said there was nothing to talk about. In the end Helen and Ed divorced.

Husband wanted. Apply within

Stan and Shirley ran a family business. Shirley kept the books and ran the office. One day she noticed, when she was reviewing the company's telephone statements, that quite a few calls had been made to a particular number in another city.

When Stan returned to the office that afternoon, she brought the matter to his attention. "We're doing a lot of business with ABC Company," he responded.

Shirley was aware of that, because Stan had been in Dallas often on business for two or three days at a time in the past six months. As she was leaving the office to go home, it occurred to her: the phone calls, the business trips. Was Stan having an affair? No, she told herself. They'd been married for twenty-five years. Their kids were all grown up and they had grandchildren. They were planning their retirement. They were going to sell the business and travel, something they'd always wanted to do.

But Shirley, being Shirley, confronted Stan anyway: "Are you having an affair?" Stan refused to answer. "Is that why you've been calling Dallas so often?" she questioned. Stan admitted that he was having an affair.

Shirley called time-out in their relationship. Nothing was said for the next week about the affair.

Dan P. McAdams, in his book *In Intimacy: The Need to Be Close*, cites a questionnaire conducted by Clyde and Susan Hendrick entitled "Attitudes About Love and Sex." They asked people to consider their "current love partner" or if they were not "in love" at present, a love partner of the past. Their analysis of hundreds of responses yielded six basic dimensions of romantic love: *eros*, or passionate, sexual love; *ludus*, or love as coy game-playing; *storge*, which encompasses friendship and caring; *pragma*, a practical and logical approach to love; *mania*, or dependent and jealous love; and *agape*, or selfless, altruistic love. This breakdown is like a periodic table of loving. Each of our love affairs, they maintain, is like a chemical compound containing some proportion of each of the six love elements.

What was the chemical mix of Shirley and Stan's marriage? Well, Shirley still loved him and wanted to win him back. So she posted a notice on the back door of their home: Husband wanted. Apply within.

The next day, Shirley received a letter by courier. It was a response from Stan requesting an interview at Shirley's convenience. Shirley left a note for Stan saying that she was reviewing the applications and would be in touch in a few days. An appointment was made to discuss the opportunity over dinner a week later. They considered the details of the "job description" and Shirley offered Stan the job. Stan accepted.

Time-out gave them a fresh beginning in their relationship. The affair ended — that was one of the requirements of the new job. And their relationship was reestablished with more devotion and respect than they had ever experienced.

An article in the November 5, 1990, issue of *Newsweek* caught my eye. "For Longer Life, Take a Wife: A New Study Examines Marriage and Mortality." A team of researchers from the University of California, San Francisco, reported that middle-aged men without wives were actually twice as likely to die during a ten-year span as men with wives. Subjects who shared living quarters with people other than a spouse had the same lower survival rates as those who lived by themselves. "The critical factor," says Maradee A. Davis, associate professor of epidemiology and biostatistics, who headed up the study, "seems to be the presence of a spouse." The lower survival rates for the spouseless were found primarily in men who were widowed, separated or divorced, rather than in those who had never been married. Married men reported a significantly higher level of well-being than those who weren't married, perhaps because they are cared for by nurturing wives.

Marriage Checkup

Good marriages don't just happen. You have to work at keeping the vows you made to each other on your wedding day.

Gloria May, a registered marriage and family therapist, says that "to be intimate with another person, we have to be intimate with ourselves first. This requires a deep understanding and acceptance of our good and bad points, confronting ourselves as we really are and accepting our-selves completely, the shadow side too, and coming out on the other side, feeling that, despite everything, we are lovable and worthy . . . Ultimately it's self-assurance and self-acceptance that gives us the courage to endure the risk in intimate relationships."

What are the warning signs of a marriage in trouble? When you don't have fun together. When your partner doesn't accept you as you are. When you have a feeling of discomfort between you. When you feel uncomfortable in the patterns but can't seem to break them. When your disagreements are more frequent and escalating. When your decision-making process is distorted.

One of the most effective methods you can use to keep your marriage on track, heading in the direction you want it to go, is to have a marriage checkup. It's a fantastic opportunity to do a little preventive maintenance. It can make a world of difference to your relationship and save you a lot of agony over the short and long term.

On your anniversary, celebrate your union not only with a special dinner or weekend away (do I hear week-in-the-sun?), but with a marriage checkup. It's not all that painful and can be just what the doctor ordered.

The couple that best illustrates this idea is Brad and Jan. Every year of their eleven-year marriage they have made a point of taking time-out for a marriage checkup. They make an appointment with an excellent counselor who asks questions about their marriage — just as a medical doctor would do an annual physical. How are you getting along? Are you experiencing any difficulties? Do you have any complaints you'd like to register or talk about? How are you growing? What lies ahead?

The interview lasts for about an hour and a half. Both

Brad and Jan say that the checkup helps them to clarify direction, puts them back in touch with each other in positive ways, gives them clues to deal with their problems and generally lets them know that their relationship is worth the time and effort.

William Betcher and Robie Macauley, in their book *The Seven Basic Quarrels of Marriage: Recognize, Defuse, Negotiate and Resolve Your Conflicts*, suggest the basic quarrels concern gender, loyalties, money, power, sex, privacy and children.

Blaine Fowers and Dr. David Olson, family psychologist and director of a marriage-counseling program called Prepare/Enrich, found that the age of the marital partners makes a difference: men and women in their twenties largely wanted an egalitarian marriage; couples in their thirties were more frequently divided over their roles, with wives more likely to demand equality and husbands more likely to insist on love, honor and obey; older couples, generally speaking, were satisfied with the traditional pattern.

Dr. Howard Markman, director of a center for marital and family studies at the University of Denver, concludes that money, sex and power are still the "big three" causes of concern, the ones at the top of his list after fifteen years of study. The sources of disagreement are the same, but the emphasis has changed with higher expectations.

A marriage checkup is like a well visit. Brad and Jan have the usual problems any couple experiences: too much month and not enough money, static on the line that disrupts their communication, determining priorities. But the checkups help.

Can a marriage checkup work for you? It's certainly worth a try.

Altared decisions

Everything was ready for the big day. The cars. The church. The flowers. The reception. The honeymoon. For months Mary and Ted and their families had been hard at work planning what sometimes appeared to be the wedding of the century. Move over, Charles and Di!

It was rehearsal night and the wedding party was preparing for the ceremony and anticipating the next day's festivities. After the rehearsal, the bride and groom asked to speak to me privately. They were concerned about feeling so nervous before their wedding. They thought it was rather strange that, after living together for two years, both of them would have misgivings about going through with their wedding.

I told them it was never too late to change their minds. The sky wouldn't fall if they didn't get married. I said that either one of them could call me in the morning if they wanted to talk some more. Barring that, I told the bride that if she decided not to get married, to give me a really big wink before she came down the aisle. A little warning for me to change gears. They went off to their post-rehearsal party.

I didn't hear from them the next morning and figured that they'd worked things out.

The organ was playing when I entered the sanctuary with

Ted and his best man. On cue, Mary appeared opposite me at the end of the aisle.

She winked. One eye, then the other. And I knew. When she arrived at the altar, she joined Ted. Both of them winked at me. I indicated to the guests that there was an unforeseen detail that had to be attended to. Then, the bride and groom and their parents followed me into a small adjoining room.

Ted and Mary called time-out. They came to the realization that, although they cared very much about each other, they didn't love each other enough to spend a lifetime together. So they canceled their wedding ceremony and called off their marriage. The guests were invited to the reception to celebrate friendship and family.

Sometimes it takes tremendous courage to call time-out. Today both Ted and Mary are happily married — to other people.

I'm outta here!

Denise looked in the mirror. What she saw wasn't pretty. Last night her husband had "lost it" and beaten her up. It wasn't the first time. But this time, Denise felt differently about it. As she stood there staring through swollen eyes at her bruised face and body, she declared, "I'm not going to take this anymore! I'm outta here!"

Denise called time-out.

Linda McLeod, in her book *Wife-Battering in Canada: The Vicious Circle*, points out that one in ten women is beaten by her partner. Wife assault is responsible for sixty percent of all female murders in Canada. Abuse happens to women of all income and educational levels, in all religious and ethnic groups. Between two and six million women are battered each year, according to the National Coalition Against Domestic Violence (NCADV). According to the Bureau of Justice statistics, three in four victims of spouse abuse were divorced or separated at the time of the abuse.

Married for nine years, Denise and Chuck had two children, four and six. The physical abuse started right after the birth of their first child and grew progressively worse. Denise lived in constant fear. The beatings became more frequent and more severe, with no apparent reason, and were usually alcohol-related.

Ignoring a beating is a dangerous mistake. So consider the first beating a danger signal. You have several options: leave temporarily; leave permanently; stay and hope your partner will change. If you decide to leave, take your children to avoid later custody problems, take your money, address book and identification, and if you have time, take clothing and personal belongings.

Denise feared for her children's safety and her own. Spouse abuse has been identified as a major precipitating factor in cases of female alcohol and drug abuse, child abuse, attempted suicide and situational disorders.

According to a 1988 study by the U.S. Department of Health and Human Services, more than one million children a year are victims of child abuse and neglect, an increase of two-thirds above 1980 estimates. About half of the cases involve abuse, physical, sexual or emotional. The other half involve neglect, either of a child's physical needs or of his or her educational and emotional needs.

No one would ever have suspected that Chuck abused Denise, because at work and in the community, he was a "really nice guy." But in reality, he was Dr. Jekyll and Mr. Hyde. Chuck had not talked about it with Denise, but she knew from his sister that when he was a child he was beaten by his father.

For Denise, the past five years had been like walking on eggshells all the time. Chuck needed to control her and kept her off balance. She felt like a hostage in her own home. Chuck would put tape on the door so she wouldn't leave. If she did he would know. There was constant verbal abuse, as well, and Denise's self-esteem hit rock bottom. Occasionally she would think, in the midst of this hell, that maybe she was to blame.

But that morning in front of the mirror, Denise called time-out and broke the vicious cycle. She planned her getaway carefully. Four weeks later she and her two children went to a women's shelter near Toronto, Ontario. There, she was supported and affirmed, and she found temporary safety for herself and her children, away from her husband.

Although she wanted to end the violence and not the relationship, Chuck was not ready to seek the help he needed. However, there are an increasing number of men who *are* getting professional help. In the Duluth Abuse Intervention Project, one out of every nine or ten adult men has been ordered into a rehabilitation program for wife abusers. In Calgary, Alberta, there is a program that provides early intervention, and men can receive assistance within forty-eight hours to halt the cycle of violence and make homes safer for women. Most men do love their families and feel badly about any abuse that has occurred.

Chuck and Denise are now separated and will probably divorce. Denise and the kids are safe and happy, although they miss their father. And Chuck? Well, he's still angry.

CHAPTER 6

Time-Out for Your Family Life

FAMILY STRESSES AFFECT performance in the workplace. A survey of thirty thousand employees in the United States showed seventy-one percent of respondents experienced stress from work and family conflicts; almost half felt that stress resulting from those conflicts affected their work. And Statistics Canada reports that people were absent from work for personal or family reasons twice as often in 1987 as in 1977.

In 1987, the Family Unity Week Committee of Red Deer, Alberta, a coalition of representatives from business, industry, unions, churches and social agencies working together to promote positive family life, commissioned a study on how workplace and family affect each other. In the study, employees stated that the first and most pressing need was time. There was not enough time outside of work to satisfy the demands of the family and to meet personal needs. The next highest concern was attending to the needs of children. These needs included high-quality, affordable child care for sick children; time to join children in their activities; and time for household chores and family enjoyment. Respondents reported needing more time during working hours to fulfill family responsibilities.

Employers stated that employees with families are more stable and committed than others. However, employers have concerns about absenteeism, decreased productivity and time off for family concerns.

The report concluded that employers should make more attempts to achieve a closer integration of work and family responsibilities, through greater workplace flexibility such as job sharing, more flexible workweeks, banked overtime, permanent part-time, flex-time, and personal or family leave options.

Your average family

Meet the Smiths. They're your average family. They're your reasonably normal family that's trying to find its way through the joys and tribulations of having teenagers. A boy and a girl. And they're mostly happy.

Parenting teenagers is a new task for Mom and Dad Smith. They were teenagers once and have some clues about what their son and daughter are going through. But today's world is different from the one they grew up in, and the expectations parents have of teens and teens have of parents are extremely high.

John, their first-born, is sixteen and has always been a compliant, nice kid. But now he's acting out, bashing authority whenever he sees the slightest opportunity. He knows everything. You can't tell him a single thing he doesn't know or hasn't an opinion about. Which makes communication with John very difficult, unless you like listening a lot. Oh yes, and he absolutely must have a car.

Alison, their fourteen-year-old daughter going on twenty-three, is declaring independence early. She has a steady boyfriend, who is, of course, not exactly Dad's first choice.

So John and Alison are growing up. The Smith family finds itself growing apart.

Mom and Dad Smith understand the need for their children, soon to become adults, to spread their wings and fly. To experiment with life and to risk. But also to know that there is always someone at home to believe in them. Not all communication had broken down.

To be supportive, Mom and Dad Smith called time-out for the family to express their own concerns about the family and also to hear John and Alison talk about their needs and concerns and how they could contribute to family life. Although there was a little initial resistance from the kids, the first family conference was convened after dinner on a Sunday evening.

Although it wasn't a roaring success, it was a good start. It became a new tradition for the Smith family. They agreed to have on the first Sunday of every month a regular time-out, a family conference, the purpose of which was to connect with one another, to communicate and to keep growing together in love. To figure out solutions together, to raise issues and concerns.

The bottom line was that each member of the family had

a special voice with a time and place to be heard. Strong bonding resulted from these family conferences and a less uptight family. There is, above all, a love for one another that builds trust and respect and provides the freedom and safety for all of them to grow and make mistakes in a compassionate, forgiving environment. A great way to use time-out to keep the family strong and healthy.

Some parents turn to Toughlove, an organization that's "a loving solution for families that are being torn apart by unacceptable adolescent behavior." In this organization's guide, *Tough Love: A Self-Help Manual for Parents Troubled by Teenage Behavior*, parents are asked if they feel the following: helpless to deal with your teenage children's behavior, victimized by your children, betrayed by your children, disappointed in yourself as a parent, you've lost control of your life, sad about your family, confused about what's happening in your family, betrayed by schools and police, blamed by everyone, frightened by the potential for violence in yourself and your children. I have witnessed some miraculous turnarounds in behavior with this compassionate program.

Single parent

A study by D. Blakenhorn in 1989-90 shows that virtually every child desires two biological parents for life and that child-rearing is most successful when it involves two biological parents, both of whom are strongly motivated to perform the task. Yes, that's the ideal, but it's not always possible.

In 1986 the traditional husband/wife family represented eighty-seven percent of all families, down five percent from 1961. Seventy percent of single-parent families were due to divorce, not widowhood.

In the eighties, single-parent households continued to be the fastest-growing type of family household. The largest increase has been in single-parent households headed by males, up fifty-seven percent between 1980 and 1988. Households headed by female single parents continued to outnumber those headed by male single parents by nearly four to one. In 1988, there were 13.3 million single-parent families in the U.S., twenty percent of all family households. By the year 2000, the proportion is expected to rise to twenty-five percent.

Julie put down her suitcase, kicked off her shoes and flopped on the bed. She could hardly believe she had two whole days for herself. Two whole days. She couldn't remember when she'd last had a couple of days to do whatever she wanted. No cooking, cleaning or children!

For the past eighteen months, she had the full responsibility of taking care of her two boys, aged five and seven. She loved them dearly. But they were a handful. They were staying with her parents while she and her sister, Andrea, recharged their batteries in the Big Apple.

For Julie, the break had come none too soon. She felt as if she was going to burst if she didn't get some relief from the pressures of making it on her own. She had no confidence problem. She knew she could do it, because she was a strong independent person. But the day-in, day-out responsibility of taking care of the kids, getting them to their soccer games and piano lessons, and helping them with school projects and, and, and . . . She was on call twenty-four hours a day and really felt the need for a break.

Karon West, former director of health education resources at Women's College Hospital in Toronto and now a private management consultant to the health-care industry, says in *Canadian Living* magazine that "we are seeing an increase in the number of women suffering from diseases thought to be associated with stress: hypertension, diabetes, heart disease, and lung and breast cancer."

For the past six years, West has conducted stress-management workshops for working mothers. To illustrate how overextended most working mothers are, West asks the women to draw a circle on a blank page and to divide it into slices representing the hours they spend daily on housework, paid work, sleep, family, friends or a hobby. Most women are surprised to see how little time they spend on their own needs and interests. She suggests that perhaps it's a matter of giving yourself permission to take time-out and relax.

Julie knew that a lot of other women in her position were certainly not as fortunate. She had a good-paying job. But some days when she got home from work, she felt as if there wasn't anything left to give. But she called up her reserves. Now, even the reserves were getting low.

That's when her sister called to see if she would like to go to New York for the weekend. So they shopped. Had dinner at a great Italian restaurant where they didn't have to cook or clean up after anyone. Caught a Broadway show. And had a massage. It was a great weekend. Julie returned to her boys. She'd regained her sanity and perspective. She felt energized to fulfill her single-parent role.

When the voice inside encourages you to take a break, take it. Everybody needs to take time-out to be refreshed.

Two careers and a toddler

Craig and Cindy had got married about two years after they graduated from college and had worked for six years before they had their son, Christopher, who was now two.

Everything was going according to the master plan. A house and a cottage, as well as shared ownership in a ski chalet. They had a great life-style too. With a full-time nanny during the week.

They were both determined to be tops in their professions and had worked hard to accomplish their goals. Only trouble was that neither felt much satisfaction in their jobs or their marriage or their family life. The pressures of time, child care and the demands of both the workplace and the family were taking their toll.

Happiness seemed so elusive! They were suffering from weekend anxiety. There were only two days to cram everything in. (Dr. Robert Glossop of the Vanier Institute of the Family has observed that "people are sharing their tiredness rather than their togetherness.")

One day, Cindy and Craig were returning in their BMW from a weekend with Craig's parents. Craig looked in the rearview mirror and saw that Christopher had finally fallen asleep in the car seat. What a precious little guy! It was hard to believe that he was two already.

For some reason or other, seeing Christopher triggered something in Craig. Craig's one regret about his own childhood was that his father had not spent much time with him. And now Craig saw himself following in his father's footsteps. He hardly knew Christopher. He was so busy pursuing his career that he was neglecting one of the best things that had ever happened to him.

William R. Mattox, Jr., a policy analyst on work and family issues for the Family Research Council, has written in an article "America's Family Time Famine" that "the children of today's overextended parents are starving — starving from a lack of parental time, attention and affection."

Parents today spend forty percent less time with their children than did their parents in 1965, according to data that sociologist John Robinson of the University of Maryland collected from personal-time diaries. In 1965, parents spent approximately thirty hours a week with their kids. By 1985, parent-child interaction had dropped to just seventeen hours a week.

In roughly one-third of all two-income families today, one-half of those with preschoolers, spouses work complementary shifts to maximize the amount of time children are cared for by at least one parent. Two-income households spend considerably less time with their children than do breadwinner-homemaker households.

And if you think that buying off the kids compensates for your absence, think again. Harvard University child psychiatrist Robert Coles cautions parents not to get caught in the "teddy bear syndrome." He says, "Some of the frenzied need of children to have possessions isn't only a function of the ads they see on TV. It's a function of their hunger for what they aren't getting — their parents' time. . . . Parents are too busy spending their most precious capital — their time and their energy — struggling to keep up with MasterCard payments. They're depleted. They work long hours to barely keep up, and when they get home at the end of the day they're tired. And their kids are left with a Nintendo or a pair of Nikes or some other piece of crap. Big deal."

A *Fortune* survey of four hundred working mothers and fathers with children under twelve found that more men than women, thirty to thirty-five percent, had actually refused a new job, promotion or transfer that would have cut into their family time. Craig and Cindy realized it was time to call time-out. They were determined to establish a healthier balance between their work and their family. Together, they reassessed their priorities. Giving their marriage and family life top priority meant dropping some of their activities.

The young couple gained far more — a lasting relationship with each other, and with Christopher.

Financial crunch

Rob and Patti felt as if their whole world were falling apart as they left the bank manager's office. They had tried to persuade the bank to give them a little more time but to no avail. The bank called their loans.

Rob excelled in everything he put his mind to. He had been the top salesperson in his company for six years running. But the urge to be his own boss caused him to look at several opportunities, one of which he chose. He threw himself into this promising new venture and invested heavily.

Unfortunately there was a severe downturn in the economy that affected his business substantially. He borrowed more, hoping the upswing would come soon.

To make a long story short, the recovery came later than sooner, and Rob found himself in debt beyond his wildest nightmares. Rob and Patti had a bundle of obligations and commitments to keep. They had two kids, one in college and one in high school. They had a large mortgage on their house. And to top it all off, they had promised some assistance to Patti's mom and dad, who had retired.

The National Council on Aging reports that 2.7 million adult children are caregivers for their parents in the U.S. The majority of older Americans are cared for in their children's or in someone else's home, four times as many as cared for in nursing homes. Although the majority of caregivers to the elderly are forty-five to sixty-four years old, thirty-six percent of caregivers are themselves older than sixty-five. Seventy-two percent of all caregivers are women, twenty-nine percent of whom are daughters and fifty-five percent of whom are employed outside the home. Nearly ninety percent (1.8 million) of women have to care simultaneously for both children and parents, particularly women who put off having a baby until their late thirties.

Unfortunately, the stress and strain created by being "sandwiched" between two generations has some regrettable results. An estimated 1.1 million elderly Americans are abused annually. Nearly six in seven, or eighty-six percent, of the abused elderly are mistreated by members of their own families. One study suggests that as few as one in fourteen incidents are actually reported; most cases are reported by secondary or tertiary sources, not by the person being abused. Abuses of the elderly range from physical (assault, neglect, deprivation, rape) and psychological (verbal assaults, calculated verbal acts with intent to drive persons to insanity or suicide) to financial (provider taking money from elderly for care and then not providing care).

Rob and Patti did the wise thing. Perhaps the only thing. They called a financial-crunch time-out.

With the help of a qualified financial planner, they did a complete inventory of their assets and liabilities. But more important, they took a fresh look at their values and priorities and their life goals. They discovered that maybe some of the things they were striving to attain weren't really what they wanted. They laid out a financial plan that included consolidating their debts, selling their house and moving to more affordable housing, and finding work that provided a steady income.

Although it feels like starting from scratch, Rob and Patti are experiencing a certain stability and security that takes away some of their anxiety. The time-out helped them regain the confidence to live within their budget comfortably. Now they can breathe a little more easily.

Blended challenge

Sara and Ray fell in love. Again. Their first marriages had both ended in divorce. And now, after a lot of soul-searching, they were getting married for the second time.

The National Center for Health Statistics reports that half of all recent marriages are remarriages for one or both partners. Frank Furstenberg, Jr., a University of Pennsylvania sociologist, identifies this phenomenon as "conjugal succession." Although lifelong marriage is still an ideal, he believes that marriage has become a conditional contract.

In their book *The Blended Family*, Tom and Adrienne Frydenger offer this advice for those embarking on a second marriage: have a lengthy courting period; allow future stepchildren to fully see your shortcomings; as adults, exchange explicit goals and come to a mutual understanding of each other's expectations; don't exaggerate your future mate's qualities to your children; and clearly verbalize to the children how they fit into the new stepfamily.

There is no guarantee that a second marriage will work. Many couples have joked with me about whether I could give a marriage guarantee. I wish. Psychologist James Bray of the Baylor College of Medicine in Houston estimates that newly remarried couples face from three to ten times the stress as those in first marriages. That's because there is a multitude of new stresses, including dealing with former spouses and parents and relatives, additional financial responsibilities, child custody, alimony and visitation privileges, and communication patterns.

Statistics show that remarriages have a sixty percent divorce rate, about ten percent higher than first marriages.

For Ray and Sara married life was different this time, principally because there were children involved right from its beginning. The new instant family included Ray's two teenage children, Derek, sixteen, and Joyce, fourteen; and Sara's two children, Jason, seven, and Jennifer, four.

The difficulties of a second marriage are greater when children are involved, something on which most experts agree. About forty percent of second marriages involve stepchildren, and it appears that conflict between a stepparent and a child may be enough to destroy a family. A 1985 study of two thousand married and remarried people found that while seventeen percent of couples with stepchildren divorced during the three years of the study, only ten percent of remarried couples without stepchildren did so.

When Sara's and Ray's families got together it was under a new roof. Ray was transferred by his company to another city, so there weren't any of the usual "friendly ghosts" to contend with in the immediate neighborhood. Fortunately, there were none of the financial problems incurred by a majority of blended families, either, although there sure were more demands on the family resources.

It was a time of mega-change. The couple soon found that family dynamics are fundamentally different the second time around. Almost everything seemed new. New home. New city. New friends. New schools. New persons sharing your personal life. New customs and traditions. New disciplines. New dynamics. New ways of communicating.

In spite of all the newness, Sara and Ray got along pretty well, considering the upheaval that affected every member in a slightly different way, depending on age and maturity. Pretty well, that is, until they began to discuss when and where and with whom they would celebrate their first Christmas together. A raw nerve was struck.

Ray wanted the blended family to be alone together on Christmas Eve. His teenagers, Derek and Joyce, wanted to visit their mother and her new spouse and family. Jason and Jennifer, Sara's youngsters, didn't really know what they wanted and didn't feel much like celebrating Christmas anyhow. It just wasn't going to be the same as they remembered. Sara, well, she wished that there was a way she could postpone Christmas.

Sara and Ray called time-out — to survive Christmas in one piece and to begin the obvious work they needed to do for the long haul. They realized that there is no such thing as a perfect family and that blended families like theirs were somewhat fragile. But they were committed to making this new family relationship work.

They wisely sought professional counseling for the whole family to help the members deal with what seemed to be a mountain of issues. After much argument and lengthy discussion, they agreed to a solution that everyone could live with although everyone had to compromise a little. One thing Sara and Ray realized, as I have witnessed in my practice, is that instant family doesn't automatically produce instant love. A period of friendship is needed, a time of adjusting expectations, rearranging priorities and accommodating others, so that love may grow.

Another thing they learned in this process was to resist the temptation to group all their problems together. They uncovered a lot of unfinished business and conflicting loyalties. It takes time to disengage from a former relationship. Called the "unhooking process," it usually takes about two years, the same amount of time it takes to bond maritally.

The effects of separation and divorce vary widely from person to person, and may include sadness and depression, denial, anger, guilt, concern about abandonment, regression, and somatic symptoms. These effects, similar to reactions felt when someone close to you dies, are experienced by adults and children alike.

In her book *Helping Children of Divorce: A Handbook for Parents and Teachers*, Susan Diamond relates how a sixteen-year-old girl felt immediately upon hearing that her parents were going to divorce. "The night my parents told us, I only felt comfort from my dog. I spent the entire evening holding him in my arms and sobbing into his furry neck. He was so good. It was as if he understood. He has been the most helpful of everyone since this whole mess began."

Researchers at the National Institute of Mental Health identified the most common sources of confusion and stress for newly constituted families: names, parental authority, managing daily routines, what to praise and punish, different rules in different homes, time with children, respecting boundaries, chores and allowances.

The most problematic aspect of stepparenting is discipline. In a study of 195 families, psychologist James Bray of the Baylor College of Medicine in Houston found that the more active a disciplinary role the stepparent played, the greater the chance that the children would experience behavioral problems during the first two and a half years of the marriage. Bray found that adolescent stepchildren have significantly more problems than those in the original, intact families.

Tensions are often higher for stepdaughters, who experience a quite different relationship dynamic in a second-marriage situation. Although only eight percent of all stepchildren live with a stepfather, thirty percent of all cases of incest involve a stepfather.

Nicholas Zill, psychologist and director of the research firm Child Trends in Washington, D.C., found in a study of thirteen hundred stepchildren that they were three to five times more likely to have received psychological counseling and up to twice as likely to have failed at school.

Adult children of divorce may experience lifelong emotional damage as opposed to a short period of upset as once thought. Psychologist Judith Wallerstein, in her book *Second Chances*, concludes that into adulthood, children of divorce often suffer from a poor self-image, fear of commitment and worries about betrayal and abandonment.

Dr. Edward Beal and Gloria Hochman, in their book *Adult Children of Divorce*, suggest that two factors, economic stability and a cooperative attitude between parents who both remain active in their children's lives, can help to lessen the adverse effects on children whose parents divorce.

Time-out is an essential survival tool, and not only for families in crisis. Time-out helps them deal constructively, creatively and positively to resolve conflicts and open the doors to an honest loving family relationship.

CHAPTER 7

Time-Out in the Workplace

WORKING DAY AFTER DAY is like running a very long race — a marathon that consumes at least half your waking hours. And it can wear you down. That's why you need to take breaks regularly at work to sustain a level of peak performance and enable you to go the distance.

The "work race" does have times of intense sprinting, where you have to expend a great deal of energy in a short period. But most of the time, you must find a pace that enables you to do your job and not lose your sanity or your family in the process.

Rosabeth Moss Kanter, in her book *When Giants Learn to Dance: Mastering the Challenges of Strategy, Management, and Careers in the 1990s*, observes that "the global economy in which American business now operates is like a corporate Olympics — a series of games played all over the world with international as well as domestic competitors."

In order to rise to this tough contemporary challenge of

running in the corporate Olympics, you need to discipline yourself to take personal time-out at work.

Most companies subscribe to the philosophy that you need time to rejuvenate and catch your breath on the job. Some companies embrace the idea more enthusiastically than others, but the advantages of an alert, energetic, positive, healthy workforce are hard to dispute. Large companies, like Du Pont, as well as mid- and small-size companies, have established fitness facilities at the workplace attended by qualified personnel, or have made arrangements for membership privileges at fitness facilities in the area.

A 1989 random sample of organizations with fifty or more employees, reported on in the May 1989 issue of *Psychology Today*, found that nearly two-thirds had at least one program promoting health and that the number of such programs is on the rise. Apple Computer offers massage on the premises, sponsors an equestrian club and gives aikido lessons to help workers blow off steam. Prudential Insurance encourages its employees to take "fitbreaks" to keep sharp and open to new possibilities.

Sustain your energy by taking a walk around the block at noon. Or take a two-minute stretch break from a meeting or from sitting at a computer monitor. Just getting the oxygen flowing again will refresh you. For something a little more strenuous, try a game of squash. If your job requires air travel, I recommend getting up a couple of times during the flight and stretching your back and legs.

Find the pattern that's best for you — the rhythm of work and relaxation that energizes you for the things you have to do.

Some people use a relaxation-response technique as a way to ease tension while at work. The elements are a relatively quiet environment, a comfortable position, a repetitive mental stimulus and a passive attitude. The response is quite easily learned and can be adapted to almost any situation.

A study at Converse Inc. sponsored by the Converse Management Association found that taking relaxation-response breaks does reduce stress, as well as improve general health, performance and well-being. It also lowers blood pressure. Another U.S. survey commissioned by Converse Inc. reports that only twenty-two percent of American companies have formal dress codes. Another fifty-five percent approve of casual, sporty or less-formal styles of executive dress. Thirty-eight percent of the companies have instituted a special day of the week or month on which employees can wear casual clothes.

The weekend break is also important to the overall rhythm of your life and work. News reports confirm that the Japanese have made a significant discovery: the weekend. Tokyo has announced that it will introduce a mandatory five-day workweek for public employees. Why? Because of foreign pressures, and because the younger generation refuses to bow to the same constraints as their forebears. By December 1990, about two-thirds of private companies had brought in a five-day week at least once a month, according to a labor ministry survey. Of these companies, eleven and a half percent had the system every week.

Everyone needs breaks. Take the ones that can help you go the distance.

Somewhere out west

In *Alice in Wonderland,* Alice asks the Mad Hatter for directions. He, in turn, asks her where she wants to go. Alice replies that she doesn't know. The Hatter insightfully suggests, "Then any direction will do."

In business today, not just any direction will do. Whether you operate a one-person business from your home or are part of an international corporation, you need to know where you're headed in your work. The very best companies, I have discovered, have a crystal-clear picture of where they're going. They create the future rather than project the past. And invariably, time-out is the strategy they use to invent their future, to paint their coming corporate picture. The chief task they face is to articulate their values and establish purpose.

Values give meaning to work. A hierarchy of values gives the organization a sense of meaning, or of justification in a moral sense. It has to do with how you will travel the road in the chosen direction, or toward the desired achievements. The value system of an organization is primary, because it guides the selection of basic goals.

Purpose gives direction. A hierarchy of purpose provides the organization with a sense of direction, or desired achievements, or results. It has to do with where we are to go, or what we will attempt to achieve.

The benefits reaped by a company taking time-out to articulate its values and establish its purpose is nicely illustrated by a major multinational firm that merged with another firm.

Ever since the merger had been finalized, after months of intense discussions and negotiations, the pace had been hectic. There were so many issues to resolve. Integrating the two cultures was a bigger job than anyone had imagined. Restructuring had been fairly successful, but the different styles of operation of the two previously separate entities were still very much alive and kicking. There were two distinct corporate cultures and agendas to integrate.

Everybody was busy, busy, busy, trying to make the merger work and keep their jobs. Many executives and middle managers, as well as support staff, had been released, because the aim of the merger was to make the operation lean and mean.

Only trouble was that, in spite of the busyness, nobody really understood where they were headed. I interviewed people throughout the organization. No one, from top to bottom, knew where the operation was headed. There was a only a vague, fuzzy idea of a future destination. It was as if they were traveling "somewhere out west," but couldn't point out on the map precisely where they were going.

Whenever you go to the airline ticket counter and ask for a ticket "somewhere out west," you take your chances. In fact, you leave your destination in the hands of someone else. There are lots of places to go out west. But how far west? North or south? Vancouver or Los Angeles?

The newly appointed president called time-out. He called it first for himself, then for the executive team, and then for all the associates.

His first action was to fulfill his role as leader and determine where he wanted to lead the newly merged firm.

He met with me, in my capacity as leadership coach, one day a week for three weeks to get his own act together. Then he met with his executive team, along with me, to get their input and to define the corporate values and purpose.

The executive team met offsite to do its work on the company's future. Although there was time built in to the agenda for relaxation, the meeting got right down to business. The team's obvious conscientious work during its time-out was evident in a later meeting that presented a statement of the company's values and celebrated the company's new vision. Everybody everywhere in the operation had the same picture of where they were headed. Although there was some resistance at first, which is to be expected, people committed themselves to reaching their new corporate destination.

David Beatty, president of Weston Foods Ltd., also is persuaded of the value of taking time to determine direction. "When I analyze my time, it's unbelievably fragmented. Neither I nor my executives have ten straight hours here at the office to spend figuring out what we all mean by 'continuous improvement,'" says Beatty. "But I do know we have to get at it at some point. If it's to pull together and coordinate so we all know where we're going and how we're going to get there, we don't have time not to have time."

Not everyone is comfortable exploring the future, the realm of the "not yet." But an interest in the future is profitable in many ways. *Psychology Today* reported that personal annual income goes up as future orientation increases, and down as present orientation becomes more dominant. (It also points out that men are more likely than women to focus on the future, a tendency that increases with age.)

As it was for the company undergoing the rigors of a merger, offsite meetings are great for discussing future orientation. In her article "An Outside Chance," published in *Destinations* magazine in October 1991, Wendy Trueman reports that corporate getaways are different than they once were: "Now they're tightly budgeted, carefully focused affairs, custom-tailored to suit a particular purpose, whether it's to ensure that everybody's on the same corporate track, to figure out how to best downsize or restructure, or to expose employees to foreign markets."

Dave Clark, head of Campbell Soup, maintains that whatever you're trying to do, the act of getting up and out of your office gives you perspective. "Getting away," says Clark, "is the only way to turn off the day-to-day firefighting mentality that most of us are trapped in ninety percent of the time . . . The more remote the location and the more removed you are from the trappings of your normal work environment and personal life, the better perspective you get."

For the past four years, Northern Telecom, a global company with products sold in ninety countries, has sent its employees, from secretaries and production workers to middle managers, on two- and three-week research trips around the world to see their customers in action, and their competition. The program was initiated by former president Robert Ferchat.

The grueling sixteen-day trip was no holiday for thirty-seven-year-old Mimi Renshaw. "There was so much information to absorb," she reported. "I could have slept standing up sometimes." The seventeen-year veteran of Nortel's office in Toronto, Ontario, attended a few days of meetings in Washington and Memphis before heading south for Mexico. She describes it as one of the most important learning experiences of her life. "I found out so much about the business. I take it far more seriously now, and I realize life doesn't stop inside these walls."

Time-out is a great way to inject new life and purpose into an old or new operation. It establishes a clear sense of where the company is headed so that everybody everywhere is committed.

Sales take a dip

The graph on the wall told the story. The previous months had not been too bad, but September was a different story. Sales had slid seventeen percent.

The company, a car dealership, needed to deal honestly with its situation. The staff needed to analyze the problem, focus on the reestablished goal and develop a strategic plan to get back on track.

So the dealership was wheeled into the critical car care unit. Time-out was called for the staff of sixty-eight. They always met as an entire body once a month, but the situation seemed serious enough to warrant a meeting to deal specifically with the dramatic drop in sales.

A recession was in full swing, and that brought with it a dynamic familiar to most of the staff. A previous recession had taught them valuable lessons about how to deal with downturns in the market. One of the main things they'd learned seemed simple and obvious: after every downturn, there is an upturn. Aware of the cyclical nature of their business, they knew that before too long things would begin to improve. But in the meantime, what should they do?

Before the meeting, everyone on the staff was consulted. Involving them all in the process was valuable, giving them ownership of the recovery — their own recovery.

A Priority Management Survey concludes that "companies will also have to offer employees much more than a job and title in the 1990s. Successful companies will likely adopt the Value-Added Workplace. 'Value-Added' can be defined as a milieu that takes into account the personal, physical, social and family obligations of employees. Increasingly, employees will seek out companies that offer flexible hours, child care, and health and physical wellness benefits. To overcome stress, we expect individuals to look for greater control over how they perform their jobs. Self-improvement programs for personal growth, coping or self-management skill development will be offered as benefits in the Value-Added Workplace."

The Conference Board of Canada reports that firms bringing in alternative work arrangements reported decreases in absenteeism, tardiness and turnover, as well as increases in work quality, productivity and morale.

The time-out the car dealership took lasted for forty-five minutes and followed a prepared agenda that considered ideas and concerns gathered in the prior survey of the staff. Some of the suggestions were acted on immediately, and the staff was confident that management was not only listening but willing to take their proposals seriously.

A need for teamwork was evident, and a training program was initiated to use the slow period to get the staff working better as a team to improve the quality of service throughout the dealership. The managers went on a two-day coaching seminar, and the whole staff took a team-building day together offsite.

The time-out produced a more cohesive team and a good feeling of working together toward the same goals. The quality of service improved. And the bottom line: their concentrated, targeted efforts with a strategic plan produced increased sales, in spite of the recession.

Meetings, bloody meetings

I received an invitation to present a keynote address at a corporate conference. When I inquired about the theme of the conference, so that I could customize my remarks to support it, the response was that I could choose whatever topic I wanted. I had forty-five minutes. I pressed gently and asked if I could be given a hint of direction. The response was revealing: the company's managers always meet the second week of November.

When I met with their small planning committee, I discovered that this company's culture had an addiction to meeting. The committee members estimated that about sixty percent of each day was spent in meetings and another ten percent in preparing for meetings.

The law of diminishing returns definitely applies to

meetings. Once a point has been reached in a task, only slight improvement will be realized in relation to the time spent.

The committee members noted that often they really didn't need to meet anyway. (According to a survey by Accountemps, a temporary-personnel service, business persons waste an average of one hour and twelve minutes a day, that's two months a year, attending unnecessary meetings.) They rarely started or finished on time. In fact two of the five-member planning committee arrived late for the meeting, having been detained at other meetings. One of the members left early to attend still another meeting.

I sensed a general dissatisfaction about the way they met and suggested that perhaps the conference could focus on how to make meetings more productive, enjoyable and stimulating. Perhaps shorter. And definitely less frequent. The committee agreed.

The conference theme they chose was "Meetings, Bloody Meetings." They modeled the conference on what they thought company meetings ought to be like. My address, "We've got to stop meeting like this," set the tone for the two-day meeting, which for years had been a four-day affair.

What the planning committee gained by calling time-out was meetings that really mattered. They looked with fresh eyes at the purpose of their meeting and considered the many alternatives, including telephone and computer conferencing, as well as better written communication. In fact, in preparation for the conference, a survey of the delegates was conducted by computer and the information collected without a meeting.

How are meetings where *you* work? Maybe a quick time-out could make your meetings more productive, too.

Never enough time

Marion returned to her office after the second meeting that afternoon. She closed the door, called the message center to hold her calls and sat motionless in her chair.

Where to start? Reports to write. Estimates to prepare. People to call. Meetings to arrange. Employee conflicts to resolve. Budgets to set. Speeches to prepare. There was never enough time.

When Alec Mackenzie, author of *The Time Trap:Managing Your Way Out*, asked people how much more time they would need to do the job they'd like to do, one out of ten said he would need ten percent more, four said twenty-five percent, and the remaining half said fifty percent.

What Marion did unconsciously, by closing her door and holding all calls, was to declare time-out from the demands that face all leaders and managers, supervisors and workers — do more with less, faster with fewer, better than ever, now! This paradox was the real challenge that faced her.

The stress and frustration she was experiencing triggered her to take time-out to refocus and recall the basics of time management. Or more accurately put, the basics of self-management about time. She needed to slow down the action to remind herself of what she already knew.

She got up from her desk and dug out the notes from a seminar on time management she had attended four years before. The three words that helped her most then, she recalled, were organize, prioritize, delegate. Just glancing through her notes helped her make connections with her current situation and provided her with insights into the real purpose of her job and what was the best way to achieve it.

The time crunch is a corporate reality today. The expectation is that business will respond to customer needs with record speed. Using just-in-time (JIT) principles and techniques, Westinghouse slashed the time needed to handle an electrical-parts order from twenty-eight hours to ten minutes, and the cost per order by two-thirds. Motorola used to take weeks to make pagers. Now, using the same JIT principles, it takes two hours from order to shipment, a three hundred percent cut in cycle time, and comparable cost saving. Toyota, the godparent of JIT, plans to be able to deliver an individually specified car to a buyer in Tokyo two days after the order, a week to customers in the rest of Japan.

Marion's time-out brought a sense of order to her work, which resulted in her managing time instead of time managing her. She had less stress personally and a more efficient, productive office. She now takes an hour of time-out at the end of each week to review the past week and to plan her agenda for the next. It makes sense. Not to mention profit.

Everybody on the bus

What gets rewarded gets done. That's the focus of a book by Michael LeBoeuf called *The Greatest Management Principle in the World*. LeBoeuf often tells a legendary story to make his point:

A fisherman was out in his boat one day when he heard a tapping noise on the side of the boat. He looked over and saw a snake with a frog in its mouth. Having pity on the frog, he took his flask and poured a little wine in the snake's mouth. The snake enjoyed the wine and let the frog go. The frog was happy. The snake was happy. And the fisherman was happy. A little while later, the fisherman heard another tapping noise on the side of the boat. He glanced over and there was the same snake. This time with two frogs in its mouth.

What gets rewarded gets done! Rewarding people for performance results in pride in themselves personally, in each other and in their company. They feel good about what they accomplish together. With a unified commitment to their goals, they also build on their success.

When Jennifer's branch office had performed exceptionally well during a challenging period of transition, she decided to reward her people appropriately. She invited the staff to come casually dressed to work the following Tuesday and have lunch together to celebrate their success. The afternoon, she said, would be spent reviewing the last period and planning for the future.

At the lunch, Jennifer praised them for their efforts and accomplishments that had produced remarkable results. When she concluded her remarks, she handed out congratulatory T-shirts with the company logo on the front and their individual names on the back. Baseball caps, too. Then the surprise. She announced, "Everybody on the bus!" She had arranged for a bus to take her entire staff to a major-league baseball game and had their group picture, taken at lunch, flashed on the giant screen at the ballpark.

TIME-OUT!

You don't have to take your staff to a baseball game to reward them. It's the action of acknowledging effort and performance that's the key. Celebrating their achievement, recognizing their accomplishments, giving praise, is the foundation for building future success. It's a time-out investment that pays good dividends.

CHAPTER 8

Time-Out for Your Career

MORE AND MORE people are taking an extended time-out to stay on track in their careers, especially if they're on the fast track.

They're opting for a sabbatical, from the Hebrew *shabbath*, which means to rest.

Jim Christie and his wife, Janet Aitken-Christie, recently spent fourteen months on sabbatical — at their cottage in Ontario, in Hawaii, and on an extended motoring trip across the United States and Europe. "It's given me a new perspective on work," says Christie, a Toronto grade-school principal. "Now I'm not letting the job get to me."

"One of the big benefits," adds Aitken-Christie, vice-principal at another school, "was we had time to get to know each other."

Give me a break

Some sabbaticals are relatively brief, a few weeks or a couple of months. Artists, writers and composers in need of rejuvenation sometimes go to the MacDowell Colony, a 450-acre retreat established in 1907 in Peterborough, New Hampshire, by American composer Edward MacDowell and his wife, Marian.

What are the most stressful occupations? In a study by J. Paul Leigh, a professor of economics at San Jose State University in California, based on measurements of their blood pressure, bartenders are at a higher risk of heart attack than those in other occupations. Ranked behind bartenders are laundry and dry-cleaning operators, public administrators, food-service workers, private child-care workers, bus drivers, freight handlers, structural metal craftsmen and telephone operators.

The American Institute of Stress, looking at such factors as job demands, work pace and the need for constant vigilance, considers these the most stressful jobs: inner-city high-school teacher, police officer, miner, air traffic controller, medical intern, stockbroker, journalist, customer service/complaint worker, waiter and secretary. The least stressful jobs: forester, bookbinder, telephone line worker, toolmaker, millwright, repairperson, civil engineer, therapist, natural scientist and sales representative.

Sabbaticals are a requirement in academia so that professors can pursue research or travel. Such a break from the routine every few years keeps them abreast of new developments in their field of study and also gives them a break from the rigorous demands of teaching. Quite often they go to other universities as visiting lecturers.

Sabbaticals are becoming more popular in the business world. Companies that pay workers to take time-out are finding that employees pay back the investment with hard work, creativity and loyalty, a valued commodity in days of the disappearing company loyalist.

Junichi Yoshikawa, a forty-three-year-old plant manager with the Japanese electronics firm, Omron, took a three-month sabbatical. He decided to travel overseas, practice golf and start his own consulting and sales firm in Japan, and he tackled each with great determination. First he went to San Francisco and Los Angeles for two weeks. He played some golf and studied regulations for starting a business, and registered a company. "After two months off, I felt different. I felt I could be more creative and break away from reality."

Bonnie Miller Rubin simply ran out of energy. A journalist for fifteen years, writing about other peoples' adventures, she felt the need to recharge her batteries. She took a sabbatical, an unpaid leave from the *Minneapolis Star-Tribune* with her architect-husband, David, and their son, Michael.

In all they took eight months off. For six months they lived on a kibbutz in Israel and toured Europe for the remaining two. One of the results of Bonnie's sabbatical was an excellent book on the subject: *Time Out: How to Take a Year (More or Less) Off without Jeopardizing Your Job, Your Family or Your Bank Account.* She reports that she returned to her work reenergized, her life in better balance and more time carved out of her busy schedule for her family.

"Sabbaticals are a way for people to renew themselves, to prevent burnout," says Phyllis Wilkinson, manager of human resources at Tandem Computers Canada Ltd. She knows from personal and professional experience that "it's good for people to spend an extended period completely away from work, especially with their family." To qualify for a Tandem sabbatical of six weeks, an employee must have completed four years' service. The person can then add the six weeks to the standard two weeks' vacation.

Sabbaticals may not be possible for everyone. But there's no doubt in my mind that taking a year off from the grind will be commonplace, especially for senior leaders, in the near future.

Turning point

Why do people change careers? Why do they often give up well-established positions and careers to pursue other interests?

Some switch to increase their income. Others see a new challenge that stimulates them. Others are bored with whatever they're doing and become restless for something new or different. One thing in common to most people who switch careers is a turning point, maybe an event or a person they encounter, or a movie they see that prompts them to follow a different vocational path.

In *Modern Madness: The Emotional Fallout of Success*, psychiatrist Douglas LaBier, arguing for a balanced life, believes that people with money and power who report dissatisfaction, anxiety and physical problems, suffer from a lack of fulfillment. The trouble stems from conflict caused by compromises and trade-offs that must be made in pursuit of a successful career.

I am persuaded that many more have these turning points, but for a variety of reasons, mostly fear, they continue what they're doing. Many have expressed to me, in their later years, their deep regret at not having followed their inner signals to risk vocationally. But many do.

Gene Estess had a lucrative career on Wall Street and few financial concerns. He was an investment banker with a prestigious firm. One evening while he waited for a commuter train in Grand Central Station, he encountered Patricia, a bag lady, and her black poodle. The image of a person needing help stuck in his mind. Six years later he quit his job to focus on helping the less fortunate.

He now heads up the Jericho Project, a halfway house whose aim is to turn welfare recipients into taxpayers. "Money doesn't cure anything," he said. "I've read about too many sad, sick, wealthy people." The Jericho Project provides accommodation for those recovering from substance abuse and helps them to become worthy members of society.

Gene has few regrets about leaving Wall Street, even though it meant a substantial cut in his income. He's following his passion, doing what he loves and loving what he's doing. He's rich now — in spirit.

Le Anne Schreiber, who holds a master's degree from Stanford and a graduate fellowship at Harvard, came to New York City in the early seventies as a writer for *Time*. Her coverage of the 1976 Olympics led to a job as editor-in-chief of Billie Jean King's magazine *Women Sports*. Within eight months of joining the *New York Times*, she became the first woman to run its sports department. Two years of "prodding a herd of jock journalists" led her to a discovery that "there was nothing I wanted to do less than spend eighty hours a week administering a staff of fifty-nine men and one woman in producing three editions a day." So she became deputy editor with the *New York Times Book Review*.

In 1985, single and approaching forty, Schreiber left Manhattan for a trout stream in upstate New York. The scene was set for a life of house renovation, fishing, reading and writing. However, shortly after moving there, she received news that her mother was dying of cancer. That was a major turning point for her, and the genesis of *Midstream: The Story of a Mother's Death and a Daughter's Renewal*, a book she wrote in journal form, in which she recounts how she balances her new life against her mother's death. She makes honest observations and deep connections as she cares for her dying parent.

Tom Monahan, now fifty-four, turned his Ann Arbor–based Domino's Pizza into the world's largest pizza-delivery operation. Its 1990 sales reached $2.65 billion, and his personal fortune is estimated at $1 billion. One of his dreams was to play shortstop for the Detroit Tigers. He didn't realize that dream but did buy the team in 1983 for $53 million.

But now he's searching for something less and something more. He's been trying to sell his pizza empire so that he can devote more time to a singular cause. "I've always been a frustrated priest," he confesses. "I want to devote the rest of my life to somehow do some good." He might have followed that instinct earlier, but in grade ten, his desire to become a Catholic cleric was cooled by a rector at a preparatory seminary in Grand Rapids, Michigan, who indicated that in his opinion, Monahan "didn't have a vocation."

"The Catholic Church has exactly what this country needs," Monahan says. "The country is in bad shape today, and it stems from the destruction of the family, which is a result of a lack of religion."

His journey from "pepperoni to piety" has involved the founding of a small and exclusive group of business executives who share his rigorously orthodox Roman Catholic faith. He decided to start the group, called Legatus, Latin for "ambassador," a few hours after meeting the Pope. The group has not taken on any particular project or special causes beyond the communal desire "to be faithful to the Holy Father, Pope John Paul II, and the teachings of the church."

Formed in 1987, Legatus now includes about seven hundred practicing Catholic CEOs in eleven U.S. chapters, and three more in Canada, Mexico and Honduras. Monahan contributes about $500,000 a year in staff salaries and expenses related to travel and the publication of a newsletter.

Amy Saltzman writes in *Downshifting: Reinventing Success on a Slower Track* that many Americans are abandoning high-stress, high-salary jobs and opting for a simpler life. Those whose eighties' watchwords were work, achievement and consumption now seek closer family ties, a stronger community sense and more leisure time.

Saltzman identifies five basic types of downshifter: the "plateauer," who holds on to an interesting, comfortable position by turning down promotions and other opportunities for advancement; the "backtracker," who moves down the career ladder within an organization or profession; the "career-shifter," who transfers to a related job at a government, academic or nonprofit institution, where the work involves less time and pressure; the "self-employer," who uses skills developed on the fast track to build a business with more desirable working hours and location; the "urban escapee," who follows the same career path as before, but in a smaller center, where the cost of living is lower and the pace more relaxed.

You're fired

Jeff could see it coming. The company he had worked for so loyally for ten years was downsizing. Again.

He tried not to think about it. But he thought this was going to be it for him. He was suffering from what might be termed "ax anxiety." The recent downsizing of companies as a result of the current recession means that there are fewer levels of management to cushion the shock, and the delayering means fewer workers who, fearing for their jobs, work even harder.

The worst-case scenario fell on Jeff one Friday morning: you're fired. The letter didn't actually use the word "fired." It took a polite approach. He was classified as "redundant" in the new restructuring scheme.

Fired! A thirty-three-year-old executive, manager of training and development of McDonnell Douglas aircraft, Jeff recalls that March morning well — it was the moment he joined the ranks of the unemployed: "It was like the floor had opened up beneath me. It was like someone telling you that your mother had died or something. Ten minutes before,

I was responsible for millions of dollars, and now I had nothing but what was in my briefcase."

Jeff felt a whole range of emotions: shock, anger, fear, insecurity, dejection.

Corporate restructuring efforts, which usually take the form of downsizing, rarely come close to achieving their goals. The *Globe and Mail*'s *Report on Business* recently printed the results of a survey conducted by the Wyatt Company, international consultants. Of 1005 firms employing more than four million people, less than half the companies over the past five years succeeded in meeting cost-reduction targets; only thirty-two percent improved profits; just seventeen percent reduced bureaucracy; and a mere six percent were able to thwart takeovers.

Furthermore, fifty-three percent of the surveyed companies said that morale has plummeted among remaining workers, and thirty-seven percent of the firms reported that the effort to retain valued employees had been made more difficult. Of the restructured firms choosing to downsize, only forty-two percent began the exercise by identifying and eliminating low-value work. Instead they tended to use early-retirement programs, and so lost good performers along with the deadwood. Which explains why eighty-three percent of the surveyed firms ended up replacing some of the people they let go.

Though there have been fewer merger and acquisition transactions per year since the peak year of 1986, when 4381 deals were completed, the individual deals that have occurred have, in fact, grown larger. In 1988, 3487 transactions were completed at a record value of $226.6 billion; the value of the average transaction was twice the 1983 level.

Although hostile takeovers have generated the most publicity, they actually account for less than two percent of all announced transactions. Fully one-quarter of all deals have occurred in those industries undergoing deregulation: banking, insurance, financial services, communications and transportation.

Euphemisms are often used to disguise the real pain or reality one has to face. Other phrases I've heard or seen used in this regard include negotiated departure, skill-mix adjustment, involuntary separation, excessed, premature retirement and, my favorite, freeing up someone else's future. No matter what you call being fired, that's what it is, with all the mixed feelings and disorientation that result.

Jeff's severance package included the valuable assistance of an outplacement counselor. Through several tests and interviews, Jeff began to work things through, especially the shock and depression, which were brand-new feelings for him. He had always had a job. Other people got the ax. Not him. Until now, job security had never been one of his concerns.

His spouse felt the impact of her husband's being fired. In *I've Been Fired, Too! Coping with Your Husband's Job Loss*, authors Jill Jukes and Ruthan Rosenberg, Toronto-based reemployment consultants, recommend the following strategies to cope: don't deny your feelings — discuss how you feel with a trusted friend; if your husband is remote, remind him that the loss affects you, too, and you would like to share the burden; tell children as soon as possible, calmly and

136

straightforwardly; remind your spouse of his previous achievements; get involved in some activity of your own to escape worry; set aside time to be with each other to have fun and renew your relationship; and suggest getting professional help, especially if there is excessive drinking.

Jeff is a resilient sort of person who, once he had dealt with his initial feelings, began to see that he now truly had the opportunity to rediscover his unique skills and abilities and explore the possibilities of employment. Slowly but surely he regained his self-confidence, and as so often happens, landed a job with better pay in a field he'd always wanted to enter.

Being fired is forced time-out, to be sure. But it can dramatically and positively affect your future, set you on a better, more rewarding path.

Reentry

Caroline had mixed feelings as she sat at the kitchen table with her second cup of coffee.

She was excited that at last their youngest child was in school all day and she had the chance to pursue her career — she'd been a nurse before giving birth to her first child. But she was also feeling terribly inadequate, having been working at home and out of the job market for fourteen years. Reentering the workforce sparked both anticipation and fear.

These feelings are quite normal, according to Dr. David Lewis, psychologist for Manpower, a major British-based job-placement agency. He calls it "retrophobia," all the irrational fears people have when faced with the prospect of returning to the workplace. Dr. Lewis's studies have revealed a common pattern of four fears: techno-fear, the terror of modern office equipment; fitting-in fear, the worry about not getting along with colleagues; responsibility fear, the deep-seated angst about making a serious mistake; and keeping-up fear, a feeling of foolishness because everyone else seems to be working faster and more efficiently.

So Caroline called time-out. She took a course at a local community college that addressed the specific concerns of women reentering the workforce. This was a valuable experience, because she found that without an horrendous amount of upgrading, she could return to nursing relatively soon. She also seriously considered the possibility of starting a business in her home.

In 1988, more than seventy percent of at-home businesses were run by women. Today about sixteen million corporate employees work at home, either full- or part-time. Almost three and a half million corporate workers have formal work-at-home arrangements with their employers. Another ten million self-employed Americans operate their businesses from their homes. The total is twenty-six million at home — twenty-five percent of the American workforce.

It is estimated that three and a half million Canadian workers and thirty-four million American workers already generate some of their income from offices, workshops or studios in their homes. By the turn of the century, it is predicted that forty percent of North American workers will work from home. The corporate need to downsize and cut overhead costs, coupled with individual needs for control and independence, have created this situation.

In the end, Caroline decided to return to nursing, her first love. It reaffirmed her self-worth, gave her a new appreciation of her parenting skills as on-the-job management training, and the satisfaction that she's making a difference in the world through her contribution of energy and skills.

Work isn't fun anymore

"Are we having fun yet?" is a popular bumper sticker almost everywhere I've traveled. The question is almost universal.

In my work across North America as a speaker, seminar leader and leadership consultant, the one complaint I hear most often, from every level in the workplace, is: "Work isn't fun anymore." Which presupposes that, at some prior time, work *was* fun. But I don't think that the comment is just a nostalgic look at the past. It has more to do with the incredibly fast pace we keep, the increasing demands on us from work and family and community, and the ramifications of constant change that permeate our lives.

"In their hearts," contends John Naisbitt in *Re-inventing the Corporation: Transforming Your Job and Your Company for the New Information Society*, "people know that work should be fun and that it should be related to the other parts of their lives. People know intuitively that work should be fun. But only a few corporate innovators have created an environment in which fun, profit and productivity flow."

In a recent poll, eighty-two percent felt they were stuck in their jobs because they needed the money. The same poll reported that only ten percent of people who work do it for enjoyment. I ran across a cartoon of a man leaving his house going off to work in the morning. He walks down the sidewalk, opens the lid of the garbage can, throws in his briefcase and walks back into the house. Some days you feel just like that when work isn't fun.

Ron felt as if he were on automatic pilot. He was going through the motions of being a sales manager. He used to look forward to going to work. But now he was frustrated. There was plenty to do but something was missing. He couldn't figure out exactly what. He felt stuck in his job. And he had to find a way to get unstuck.

At dinner one evening he and his spouse were chatting. She asked him what he would most like to do in the whole world. Ron thought for a moment and responded that he would like to start his own business, be an entrepreneur, be more in control of his own destiny. "Then why don't you do it?" she asked. That caught Ron by surprise but triggered him to call a vocational time-out.

Sometimes it doesn't have to take much to spark a new thought or direction. Ron considered the advantages and disadvantages of leaving his fairly secure job, and decided in the end to follow his heart. Today he operates a thriving small business from his home. Best of all, Ron's having fun again.

In his book *Working*, Studs Terkel comments, "I think most of us are looking for a calling, not a job. Most of us, like the assembly-line worker, have jobs that are too small for our spirit. Jobs are not big enough for people."

Maybe work isn't fun for many because they have simply

forgotten how to take time off to relax away from work. I understand that even the Japanese corporations are urging employees to take some time off. "The government doesn't want people to burn out," says Hidehiko Sekizawa, executive director of the Hakuhodo Institute of Life and Living, a Japanese think tank.

Japan now has experts who advise vacationers on how to have fun: the National Recreation Association of Japan offers classes to train these "leisure counselors." About 1200 would-be advisers are currently studying ways to overcome barriers to leisure, including lack of time, money or traveling companions. The Ministry of International Trade and Industry wants corporations to have full-time "leisure advisers" to help employees plan their free time.

In an article by Humiko Makihara in *Time* magazine, Matoshi Yamada, a forty-three-year-old construction executive, is reported to have big plans for the next ten years, even though he's supposedly cutting back his activity. He wants to pass six certifying exams in such diverse fields as health and real estate, read 480 books and buy some land to build a home. After that, he intends to bicycle around the world, go to art school and volunteer his services to a Peace Corps for the elderly. In fact, Yamada's schedule is chock full until the year 2018, when he plans to buy a grave. All this meticulous planning is his way of relaxing: once a workaholic, Yamada was forced to slow down.

What's happening with your career? Are you looking for ways to increase fulfillment in your current job? Are you frustrated and considering your options? Do you have a choice? Have economic conditions forced you to search for a job that pays enough money to pay the bills, but maybe won't give any satisfaction?

A strategic break for your career, by far the most time-consuming aspect of your life, could be one of the wisest investments you ever make.

CHAPTER 9

Time-Out
for Your
Community

"FROM NOW ON," said President George Bush, "any definition of a successful life must include serving others."

Many obviously agree, because across North America, volunteerism is thriving. The Gallup organization reports that the proportion of adult Americans devoting time to "charity or social service activities" has grown steadily over the past decade, reaching thirty-nine percent in 1987. In a recent survey, ninety-two percent said it was important to "give something back" to the community. Perhaps we really are moving from the "me" to the "we" generation.

More than forty-five percent of Americans volunteered in 1987, according to a Gallup survey. The time people spent in volunteer activity increased from 3.5 hours a week in

1985 to 4.7 hours in 1987. Giving time for a specific project is growing.

Statistics Canada's recent Survey of Volunteer Activity shows that during a twelve-month period in 1986-87, an estimated 5.3 million Canadians performed volunteer work, for a total of 1.018 billion hours. The value of this volunteer work, based on an average service-sector wage, is estimated at $12 billion in 1987 (approximately $13.2 billion in 1990 dollars). The total number of hours, if converted to full-time positions, would amount to 617,000 full-time jobs. And this credit on the social ledger does not include the value of skills developed and work experience gained through volunteering.

Twenty-three million Americans are already volunteering five or more hours a week and twenty million are giving five percent or more of their income.

For businesses, giving to the community improves employee morale, makes a positive contribution to the bottom line, provides training for employees, is a low-cost, high-benefit way to get involved with community problem-solving and secure information about the community. Business retiree volunteer programs provide a natural way to stay in touch with a pool of potential consultants/part-time workers, as well as great public relations for the company.

And nonprofit organizations gain new talent and energy, new resources, fresh perspectives and renewal, low-cost solutions to problems, and the likelihood of increased giving by active volunteers.

The benefits of taking time-out to serve your community

are manifold, as I believe the examples in the rest of this chapter reveal.

For Joanna

Bonnie and Terry Jackson called time-out thirteen years ago when their daughter, Joanna, was diagnosed with diabetes. The result was a declaration: "We're going to help find a cure!"

So they set out on their journey to make their contribution of energy, resources and countless hours, especially for Joanna, but also for all who suffer from diabetes.

They connected with the Juvenile Diabetes Foundation of Canada (JDFC), a nonprofit volunteer organization whose primary mission is to find the cause, cure, treatment and prevention of diabetes and its complications.

The Juvenile Diabetes Foundation International was founded in 1970 in the United States by parents of diabetic children who were convinced that, with research, diabetes could be cured. They were determined to make that cure a reality in their children's lifetime. The purpose of the foundation is, therefore, to raise as much money as possible for diabetes research. Today the initial nucleus of dedicated families has grown to a membership in the tens of thousands, chapters from coast to coast and affiliates in ten countries around the world.

Bonnie is very active in the foundation, especially in the Toronto chapter, of which she is a past president. Terry began his volunteer work with the foundation by soliciting corporate donations with the Toronto chapter. For the past six years, he has been with JDFC, first as a board member, then as president and finally as chair of the board.

Nearly one and a half million Canadians have diabetes — a chronic disease that occurs when the body fails to produce insulin, or is unable to make use of any insulin that is present — and the number is growing by sixty thousand a year. By the year 2000, diabetes experts estimate, that rate will have risen to fourteen percent of the population from today's five percent. More than fifteen thousand have juvenile diabetes, the more serious, hereditary form of the disease. These numbers are increasing at a rate of six percent a year.

Insulin therapy only approximates the body's own insulin-producing abilities. It keeps people with juvenile diabetes alive much longer, but that's all. It doesn't prevent the disease from causing ongoing damage to the body — damage that often leads to blindness, heart attack, nerve damage, stroke, amputations and kidney failure. People with juvenile diabetes are at a particularly high risk of developing these serious complications. Because of this, diabetes is the third leading cause of death by disease in North America, after heart disease and cancer. Last year it claimed more than 450,000 lives. No wonder, then, there is so much dedication to research.

Recently, Terry Jackson was elected to serve on the board of directors of JDF International, which, since its founding, has raised a total of more than $100 million for diabetes research. The JDF mission is to make the nineties "The Decade of the Cure." Terry, with his customary optimism, is convinced that "the cure is right around the corner."

146

We hope so too, Terry and Bonnie! And Joanna and all the diabetes sufferers around the world.

Back to Africa

In 1965, when Gord Walls, a St. Thomas, Ontario, secondary-school mathematics department head and physical-education teacher, came home from a summer with Crossroads International, he vowed to return to Africa. He had spent the summer in Sierra Leone, the leader of a team of thirteen American university students building a "homemaking center for women."

Crossroads has provided many opportunities for people to take time-out for the community. It was begun in 1958 by James H. Robinson, an American clergyman who founded a program called Operation Crossroads Africa, which sent young people to work at short-term work camps in Africa. Ten years later, Canadian Crossroads International (CCI) was formed. It added countries in Asia, the South Pacific, the Caribbean, and South and Central America to its overseas program. And in 1972, it expanded when the first volunteers from the developing world came to Canada to participate in community education programs.

It wasn't until Gord was in his early sixties that he fulfilled his vow to return to Africa. A high-school principal for thirteen years, he took early retirement, and along with his spirited and determined wife, Orma, accepted a three-year foreign missionary assignment with the United Church of Canada. Gord and Orma have always had a vital religious faith and lived out their belief that "where your heart is, there will your treasure be also." Their combined heart was in their mission of generously reaching out to people who are less fortunate.

They left not knowing what they were going to face, to a new culture with a different language, not to mention a place where the risk of disease was very real. They epitomized the belief of the late Dr. Robert McClure, an extraordinary medical missionary to China who once defined adventure as "risk with a purpose."

And a great adventure it was! Their final destination and home, far away from home, was the Massai Rural Development Centre in the Ngong hills above Nairobi, Kenya.

Things didn't all go smoothly. There were times when they wondered if their work was really having an impact. Their house was broken into four times. But they were committed to helping others help themselves and sharing their talents with humanity. They not only recalled what they stood for but delivered on their beliefs with real action, action that provided life-changing strategies.

What did they gain personally from this time-out? Well, apart from at least one parasite in common, a rich experience of friendship and self-discovery. Orma, particularly, grew in self-confidence — she'd had to do a lot of public speaking, never a favorite with her, and this time it wasn't even in her own language. The couple also gained an appreciation of the tradition and culture of the Massai, with whom they had the privilege of living and working. All in all they became a lot more tolerant and understanding of others and accepting of different cultures, and when they returned to Canada, it was with an eagerness to encourage others to give of themselves to the less fortunate.

One more for the road

Cari Lightner, age thirteen, was struck and killed by a car in California. The driver was drunk at the time. Cari's mother, Candy, mourned the unfortunate death of her child, then was later appalled at the lenient penalty the driver paid. Subsequently she learned that many drunk drivers got off easy, some without ever being sent to jail.

So Candy called time-out for her community.

Angry and grieving, she founded MADD, Mothers Against Drunk Driving, in 1980, to lobby for new legislation against drunk drivers. The goal of MADD was to have safe, alcohol-free roads, in the belief that strict criminal prosecution of drunk drivers is the most effective deterrent in reducing drunk-driving victims.

Candy encountered a very bumpy road in accomplishing her goals. But after an aggressive campaign, California passed what are the toughest laws on drinking and driving in the U.S. Due to her efforts, MADD is now an international nonprofit organization with over half a million supporters and members in the U.S., Canada, Great Britain and New Zealand. Public awareness of the problem has resulted in juries being more sympathetic to the rights of the victim than to the rights of the intoxicated driver.

MADD provides support for victims of drunk drivers and continues to lobby for better drunk-driving legislation. It has been a major influence in reducing the number of drunk drivers on the road. Most important, however, MADD's presence has reduced significantly the number of traffic fatalities caused by drinking and driving.

Earth Day

Earth Day was conceived by Wisconsin Senator Gaylord Nelson and planned as a nation-wide teach-in about the environment at some fifteen hundred colleges and ten thousand other schools. Twenty million people participated in the first Earth Day in 1970.

On its twentieth anniversary, April 22, 1990, about fifty million Americans took part in about three thousand activities, from racing in San Diego's three-mile Run for the Rainforest to building nesting boxes for ducks on Chesapeake Bay. Millions more watched Earth Day specials on television.

There are two major environmental issues of the nineties: the greenhouse effect and ozone depletion. The first is a gradual increase in the average temperature of the earth, which poses what many scientists regard as the most critical environmental threat of the decade. It is believed that global warming is taking place because heat from the sun is trapped by sharp increases in atmospheric carbon dioxide, produced by the burning of wood, coal and oil as fuel, and by the slashing and burning of tropical rainforests. Rainforests are being destroyed at a rate of one acre every second — eliminating in decades what took sixty-five billion years to create.

A United Nations report released by the UN Environment Program in October 1991, the World Conservation Union and the World Wide Fund for Nature, with input from scientists from many countries, says, "We must adopt life-styles and development paths that respect and work within nature's limits. Because of the way we live today, our civilization is at risk." The report, four years in the making, set out 132 measures it says must be implemented if the planet is to remain capable of supporting its population. Ensuring the longterm survival of life on Earth, the report suggests, will cost $1,288 billion over the next decade.

The global problem must become personal, which means we have to change our habits. And we are, with reminders such as Earth Day. Many people are following the invitation to reduce, reuse and recycle. Blue Boxes for recyclable glass, paper, plastics and tins are an accepted part of life in many communities. The purchase of such environmentally friendly products as unbleached coffee filters, biodegradable soap and energy-efficient light bulbs is at least a small step in the right direction.

Nearly one-half of Americans took some kind of environmental consumer action in 1990: fifty-four percent stopped using aerosol sprays, forty-nine percent bought products made from recycled materials, thirty-four percent reduced their use of paper towels, and thirty-four percent didn't buy a product because of concern for the environment.

There are about two thousand active environmental groups worldwide. They include Greenpeace, which has four million members and whose main focus is marine biology and toxic pollution, Energy Probe and Pollution

Probe. Former Beatle Paul McCartney conducted a world tour in 1989-90, encouraging people to save the planet. Members of the Friends of the Earth environmental group, which deals with such atmospheric issues as ozone depletion and global warming, were invited to go along on the tour to provide material at each concert to help raise awareness of environmental issues.

There is reason for hope. We're taking time-out for our planet.

Monkey business

I was having dinner one Friday evening with good friends in Lancaster, Pennsylvania, when Henry Longobardi, another dinner guest, turned to me and said, "You'll have to come over to our place and meet Barney." I asked who Barney was. "Our monkey," he replied. Maybe he was just kidding, I thought.

He wasn't. On Sunday afternoon, I met Barney face-to-face — literally. What a phenomenal experience! Barney wasn't just hanging around, so to speak. He was in training. Yes, serious training. No monkey business here. He greeted me affectionately and I held him in my arms, though not without some difficulty. Barney wanted to be every-where — all at the same time.

Henry and his wife, Sue, along with their two children, Nick, thirteen, and Lauren, eleven, had explored different ways they could help others in the community. They considered several alternatives. But in the end they decided to make a substantial commitment. They became a foster family with Helping Hands, Simian Aides for the Disabled, an affiliate of the Boston University School of Medicine.

Their responsibility as a foster family involves raising a baby monkey at their home for approximately three and a half years, to make it well socialized and affectionate when placed with a quadriplegic. Raising a monkey is fun and rewarding, but it isn't easy. It's time-consuming, entails some expense and requires a considerable amount of patience.

The primary foster parent must be prepared to spend at least ten to twelve hours a day with an infant monkey until it's eight months old, and at least five hours a day thereafter. The monkey may be clinging to your arm or sleeping in an apron pocket as you go about your daily routine, or playing on the floor of the room in which you are working. Although not *quite* as time-intensive as raising a human baby, raising a capuchin monkey — the favored kind — takes *significantly* more time than raising a puppy. The time commitment means that the primary caretaker must either work at home — part-time work is okay if you receive an older monkey — or have an employer who will permit the monkey to be brought to work every day. Students and most individuals who work full-time would not be able to provide the structure young monkeys require.

The hardest part, it seems to me, is that the family has to give the monkey up when requested — usually between three and four years of age. This can be tough, because not only time and energy have been invested in raising this animal, but also a lot of love. You get very attached.

In the six months following their years with a foster family, the monkeys learn the tasks that they will perform for the quadriplegic, such as answering the door and phone, using the microwave to cook food, adjusting eye glasses and wiping the face with a cloth. At the end of their intensive training period away from the foster family, they are sent to the lucky recipient. A high degree of bonding occurs, and the monkeys are very protective of their charges. Most of all, the monkey and the quadriplegic become friends.

Fostering a monkey is a big commitment for the Longobardi family. It's a time-out that takes a lot of patience and compassion. But the knowledge that their efforts will someday enable a less-fortunate person to have a better life keeps them going, especially on those days when Barney is really monkeying around!

CHAPTER 10

Ten Time-Out Tactics

IN CHAPTER TWO I defined time-out as a principle of renewal, a discipline of growth and a strategy of control. In this final chapter, I want to suggest to you ten proven tactics that can help you get the most out of your time-outs.

Whether your time-outs are for your personal or intimate life, for your family life, for your professional life or used to benefit the community, these tactics, if practiced consistently, will release the potential that time-out has to change your life.

The tactics are general guidelines, fairly universal in nature, and must be adapted to fit your specific situation. Time-out is a very personal matter, and you will want to experiment to see just what works for you. The dictionary defines "tactic" as the act or skill of employing available means to accomplish an end. The *end* of time-out is a beginning — the point at which you restore your passion for life, love and work. These tactics will help you reach your end.

Trust your inner signals

Trust, don't fight them. Your inner signals are the most reliable source to let you know when to call time-out. Who else knows you better? Who else knows what's really happening inside you? Who else is in touch with your innermost thoughts and feelings? When your internal system recognizes your need to take time-out, it's programed to pass on the message so you can do what you need to do.

Some people get very proficient at denying their inner signals to slow down, or pay more attention to a relationship, or follow a dream. They ignore, block out, their true feelings. They gradually become deaf to their inner voice. Sometimes they pay a fatal price.

Being attentive to the strong signals from your heart will enable you to call time-out. There's no perfect time to call time-out, but when you allow yourself to receive the message your inner self is beaming, you'll be able to respond appropriately.

Trust your inner signals. They'll prompt you to review where you've been and where you're headed. They'll help you anticipate the boiling point in a family dispute or a work situation and guide you in productive, profitable ways.

Trust your inner signals. They're on your side.

Take charge

Periodically, as we have seen in the book, there are situations when time-out is called for you. You are forced to take it. You have no alternative. But most of the time you're the one who has to blow the whistle for time-out. You have to take control and responsibility for your welfare, to take charge of your life and create your own future. Healthy people draw their strength from inside, trust their signals and act on them.

The act of calling time-out is liberating and energizing in itself. Countless people have told me that the moment they called time-out, they felt a sense of relief, knowing that they were not just reacting to life but in fact creating their own future. Their self-worth and self-esteem grew simply because they acted. They discovered purpose and meaning because they were on the way.

If you fail to act, you may die with your music still in you. Take charge and get on your way to become what only you can be.

Set realistic expectations

You've called time-out. Now you have the important task of setting realistic expectations. How much can you reasonably expect to achieve in the time you have available?

Expecting too much can be demotivating, and you must guard against the tendency to believe that you can accomplish more than is humanly possible. Most of the time people overestimate what they think they can achieve.

That doesn't mean that you can't set a goal that stretches you, helps you to grow and reach new heights. But time-out is more productive if you set expectations you feel comfortable with.

The amount of time you have will dictate to some degree what you can accomplish. How much time *do* you have?

What can you deal with efficiently in that space of time? How critical is the situation? What are the priorities? The answers to these questions will help you set realistic expectations.

You've got to be patient. Rome wasn't built in a day. A marital problem that has gone on for twenty years cannot be resolved in a day, either, no matter how good the counselor is.

Set realistic expectations and you'll achieve realistic results.

Choose a conducive place

Sometimes you don't have a choice. The nature of your situation demands that you take time-out on the spot. There isn't time to go elsewhere. If you are faced with making a business decision in the next five minutes, you haven't got time to go anywhere, anyway. You do the best job you can with the time available in the place you're in.

Most of the time, though, you have at least some choice about where to hold your time-outs. A carefully chosen location can be instrumental in achieving your goals. You need a conducive place, one that can further your purposes. If you want to relax and unwind, choose a spot that will slow you down and give you the environment to release your tension and satisfy your personal need for a break.

Alexander Graham Bell, whose inventions include the iron lung, the flat-disk gramophone, the portable desalination unit, the first airplane to fly a mile and the telephone, chose a unique environment. This three-hundred-pound inventor used to do his thinking on a summer night, floating in the lake at his Nova Scotia home, totally naked except for a glowing cigar.

If your purpose is to develop a five-year business plan, then choose a place that will put your staff in an atmosphere that enables them to create your business's future.

If you're planning a family outing, choose a place where the whole family can enjoy their time together.

No one place will give you everything you want, although Hawaii may come awfully close. Usually it's a matter of striking an activity balance so that you can accomplish your goal. A balance that gives you time to sleep or play a game of tennis, go for long walks or do nothing, work at preparing a corporate strategy or have a party with music and dancing.

They say a change is as good as a rest. It might mean going to a country retreat or simply going down the hall. But choose it carefully.

Be totally present

This is the key tactic to make your time-out come alive.

It's more than showing up. It's bringing all that you are, all your potential, all your intellect, talent, skill and enthusiasm to bear on the situation at hand. The quality of being present transforms ordinary time-outs into extraordinary happenings.

Watch a major basketball team, like the L.A. Lakers, in their time-outs. Every member of the team listens intently to the coach's directions. The crowd may still be roaring, but coach and players have their minds locked into their task. Nothing distracts them. Their time is limited, so there's none to waste. Their collective energy is intensely focused. But it's not an uptight intensity.

In my experience the more critical the situation, the more chance there is of the parties involved in the time-out being totally present. But considering the pace at which we live today, being totally present is hard. To be in one place at one time mentally, physically, spiritually, totally present to the people and the situation, demands tremendous concentration. Nevertheless it is absolutely essential, to give you the full life-renewing benefit of time-out.

Focus on the future

Soren Kirkegaard once commented that "life must be lived forwards, but it must be understood backwards."

No matter how much you may wish to, you can't change the past. What's done is done. Unfortunately many people, even though they understand this reality, live their lives disregarding this fundamental truth. They keep rehearsing and repeating their pasts, complete with the failures. You can learn valuable lessons from the past, but the past was meant to remembered not relived.

The past is at one end of the life spectrum and the future at the other. Living in the present, you live between the past and the future, between memory and hope. It's an exciting tension.

Your future, unlived, with its possibilities stretching out before you, is far more important than your past. What you think you can become is far more important than what you have been. Ken Danby, the Canadian landscape artist, was asked what his best painting was. He replied, "My next one."

Appreciate your past. Start dreaming. Then get going. Create your future and live it as only you can. Focus on your future and progress toward your destination of promise.

Remain open

Time-out provides you with the opportunity to consider all the possibilities and find the best solutions to your problems and challenges. So take advantage of your time-out by remaining open to others, to their ideas and perspectives. I saw a bumper sticker that belongs to a closed-minded person: "Everybody is entitled to my opinion."

Remain open to others' opinions. That means you have a fairly well-developed sense of your own worth, strong enough to listen to other points of view. You don't have to agree with what you hear, but if you listen to another idea, you may be persuaded that your own is preferable.

Remain open to the unexpected. Allow yourself to be surprised. Experience different points of view, figuratively and literally. When I visited the Grand Canyon, I saw it from three distinctly different points of view: on the ground looking into the canyon, from the river that flows through the canyon, and from the air, overlooking the vastness of the canyon. My memory and experience of the canyon continue to be enriched by these three points of view.

Life is a learning process. Remaining open gives you the flexibility to grow and keeps open the options for development.

Think creatively

Time-outs can be much more effective, and enjoyable, if you think creatively. I believe that everyone is creative, and unleashing either an individual's or a group's creative capacity serves the purpose of the time-out.

Creativity cannot be forced. It emerges from confidence in your own self to solve a problem, find a solution, rise to a challenge or seize an opportunity. It's confidence that you can figure out how, not if, you will achieve your goal.

Thinking creatively is really just an attitude, one that comes naturally to some and is difficult to reestablish in others. From childhood, some people have had the creative impulse drained out of them little by little. As adults, they are convinced they are simply not creative, and that's that.

The best creative solutions come not when you're tense but when you're in a relaxed state of mind. Humor acts as a catalyst in this regard and opens the door to your inner resources. It opens you up to life and to ideas that you never dreamed of.

Sometimes at business conferences, I invite small breakout groups to report back to the whole session by using a song. You'd be surprised at the number of talented lyricists and performers who lurk in executive ranks. They report to me that preparing and singing the song, however silly it may have seemed at the time, helped them to think creatively.

By the way, what do you call a boomerang that won't come back?

Right. A stick.

Go with the flow

Time-out is a blend. It's a combination of directing the flow of your life and of going with the flow of your life. It's a balancing act, both dimensions essential to the process.

The former is the recognition that you have to take responsibility to change the direction of your life so that you can fulfill your personal mission; the latter is a willingness to be inspired and guided on your journey. The former is a matter of the will; the latter essentially a matter of the spirit. The former takes control; the latter yields control to a higher power that directs the natural flow of life.

Robert Fritz, in his book *The Path of Least Resistance*, talks about the natural flow of life. He suggests that once you have decided where you want to go, your destination, then your life will naturally seek out and find and direct you along the path of least resistance.

I have found this to be true in my own life. When I decided and set out on a new career, many things happened naturally to help me achieve my goals. Those who run rapids know precisely what I am referring to. The river has a natural flow that will help, not hinder, you from going where you want to go. Surfers go with the flow when they catch and ride the crest of a wave.

Time-out can put you in touch with the natural flow of your life. So you can direct the flow. And go with the flow.

Prepare for time-in

A vital part of time-out is preparing for time-in. It's the transition that you must make to cushion your landing, your reentry. The process is similar to that of a rocket reentering the atmosphere and landing on the earth.

If you don't prepare, you may find the impact of reentry overwhelming. Depending on the circumstances, your time-out will have renewed you but not for everything. Henry Kissinger wrote: "There cannot be a crisis next week. My schedule is already full."

A little planning beforehand can substantially diminish the jolt of coming back to your regular world.

Or you may find the reentry frustrating. A friend of mine took a management course in which he was encouraged to be empathetic in his management style. When he returned to his workplace, ready to practice his new management philosophy, he was reminded in the first ten seconds that he was still working for Attila the Hun.

Just as you warm up your body for a workout, warm up your mind and your heart and your body for your return. Imagine yourself handling your situation with your renewed perspective. Think through and write down your plan of action for time-in, especially your first one or two actions.

Preparing for time-in will considerably increase the value of your time-out.

Time-in!

Your time-out is over. The action resumes. And the real purpose and value of time-out are realized.

I know I don't have to convince you of the necessity of time-out. You already know that it's an essential principle of renewal, a discipline of growth and a strategy of control.

But what you do need perhaps, from time to time, is to be reminded to take it.

That's what I've tried to do in this book. Encourage you to take time-out so that you'll have a fulfilling life. I've nudged you a little. Occasionally I've tried to shock you into awareness. As Peter Drucker, a management consultant specializing in economic and business policy, once commented, "I have learned to be consultant as insultant, because people don't listen when you hint."

One of the most precious gifts we receive at birth is time. Voltaire's description of the nature of time, from his book *Zadig: A Mystery of Fate*, reflects my own beliefs:

> What, of all things in the world, is the longest and the shortest, the swiftest and the slowest, the most divisible and the most extended, the most neglected and the most regretted, without which nothing can be done, which devours all that is little, and enlivens all that is great?
>
> Time.
>
> Nothing is longer, since it is the measure of eternity.

Nothing is shorter, since it is insufficient for the accomplishment of your projects.

Nothing is more slow to one that expects, nothing more rapid to one that enjoys.

In greatness it extends to infinity, in smallness it is infinitely divisible.

All neglect it; all regret the loss of it; nothing can be done without it.

It consigns to oblivion whatever is unworthy of being transmitted to posterity, and it immortalizes such actions as are truly great.

Time is our most precious asset.

Time-out! Restoring your passion for life, love and work. It's your call!

Resources

Albrecht, Karl. *Stress and the Manager: Making It Work for You.* New York: Touchstone Books, 1986.

Beal, Edward and Gloria Hochman. *Adult Children of Divorce: Breaking the Cycle and Finding Fulfillment in Love, Marriage and Family.* New York: Delacorte Press, 1991.

Berman, Claire. *Adult Children of Divorce Speak Out: About Growing Up With and Moving Beyond Parental Divorce.* New York: Simon and Schuster, 1991.

Betcher, William and Robie Macauley. *The Seven Basic Quarrels of Marriage: Recognize, Defuse, Negotiate and Resolve Your Conflicts.* New York: Villard Books, 1990.

Bienenfeld, Florence. *Helping Your Child Succeed after Divorce.* Claremont, CA: Hunter House, 1987.

Bradshaw, John. *Homecoming: Reclaiming and Championing Your Inner Child.* New York: Bantam, 1990.

Braiker, Harriet B. *The Type "E" Woman: How to Overcome the Stress of Being Everything to Everybody.* New York: Dodd, Mead & Co., 1986.

Brod, Craig. *Technostress.* Reading, MA: Addison–Wesley, 1984.

Campbell, Joseph. *The Power of Myth.* New York: Doubleday, 1991.

Carroll, Lewis. *Alice in Wonderland.* New York: Norton, 1989.

Clubb, Angela Neumann. *Love in the Blended Family: Falling in Love with a Package Deal.* Toronto: NC Press, 1988.

Cousins, Norman. *The Anatomy of an Illness as Perceived by the Patient: Reflections on Healing and Regeneration.* New York: Norton, 1979.

Corneau, Guy. *Absent Fathers, Lost Sons: The Search for Masculine Identity.* Boston: Shambhala Publications, 1991.

Curran, Delores. *Traits of a Healthy Family.* Minneapolis, MN: Winston Press, 1983.

Diamond, Susan Arnsberg. *Helping Children of Divorce: A Handbook for Parents and Teachers.* New York: Schocken Books, 1985.

Fassel, Diane. *Working Ourselves to Death: The High Cost of Workaholism, the Rewards of Recovery*. San Francisco: Harper, 1990.

Frankl, Victor. *The Will to Meaning*. New York: NAL–Dutton, 1988.

Fritz, Robert. *The Path of Least Resistance: Learning to Become the Creative Force in Your Own Life*. New York: Fawcett, 1989.

Fromm, Erich. *To Have or To Be*. New York: Bantam, 1983.

Frydenger, Tom and Adrienne Frydenger. *The Blended Family*. New York: Revell, 1985.

Hendrix, Harville. *Getting the Love You Want: A Guide for Couples*. Toronto: Harper and Row, 1990.

James, William. *The Varieties of Religious Experience*. New York: Random, 1990.

Jukes, Jill and Ruthan Rosenberg. *I've Been Fired, Too! Coping with Your Husband's Job Loss*. Toronto: Stoddart, 1991.

Kanter, Rosabeth Moss. *When Giants Learn to Dance: Mastering the Challenges of Strategy, Management, and Careers in the 1990s*. New York: Simon and Schuster, 1989.

Keen, Sam. *The Passionate Life: Stages of Loving.* New York: Harper, 1983.

Keyes, Ralph. *Timelock: How Life Got So Hectic and What You Can Do about It.* New York: HarperCollins, 1991.

Killinger, Barbara. *Workaholics: The Respectable Addicts.* Toronto: Key Porter, 1991.

Klarreich, Samuel H. *The Stress Solution: A Rational Approach to Increasing Corporate and Personal Effectiveness.* Toronto: Key Porter, 1988.

LaBier, Douglas. *Modern Madness: The Emotional Fallout of Success.* Reading, MA: Addison-Wesley, 1985.

Lapham, Lewis H. *Money and Class in America — Notes and Observations on the Civil Religion.* Woodland Hills, CA: Weider Health and Fitness, 1988.

Lazarus, Richard. *Emotion and Adaptation.* New York: Oxford University Press, 1991.

LeBoeuf, Michael. *The Greatest Management Principle in the World.* New York: Berkley Books, 1985.

Lerner, Harriet Goldhor. *The Dance of Intimacy: A Woman's Guide to Courageous Acts of Change in Key Relationships.* New York: HarperCollins, 1990.

Mackenzie, Alec. *The Time Trap: Managing Your Way Out.* New York: AMACOM, 1972.

MacLaine, Shirley. *Going Within: A Guide for Inner Transformation.* New York: Bantam, 1989.

McAdams, Dan P. *Intimacy: The Need to Be Close.* New York: Doubleday, 1989.

McLeod, Linda. *Wife-Battering in Canada: The Vicious Circle.* Ottawa, Ontario: Canadian Advisory Council on the Status of Women, 1980.

Naisbitt, John. *Megatrends: Ten New Directions Transforming Our Lives.* New York: Warner Books, 1982.

Naisbitt, John and Patricia Aburdene. *Re-inventing the Corporation: Transforming Your Job and Your Company for the New Information Society.* New York: Warner Books, 1985.

Peck, Scott. *The Road Less Traveled: A New Psychology of Love, Traditional Values and Spiritual Growth.* New York: Simon and Schuster, 1978.

Popcorn, Faith. *The Popcorn Report: Faith Popcorn on the Future of Your Company, Your World, Your Life.* New York: Doubleday, 1991.

Rubin, Bonnie Miller. *Time Out: How to Take a Year (or More or Less) Off without Jeopardizing Your Job, Your Family or Your Bank Account*. New York: Norton, 1987.

Russell, Robert. *To Catch an Angel: Adventures in the World I Cannot See*. New York: Vanguard, 1962.

Rybczynski, Witold. *Waiting for the Weekend*. New York: Viking, 1991.

Saltzman, Amy. *Downshifting: Reinventing Success on a Slower Track*. New York: HarperCollins, 1991.

Schreiber, Le Anne. *Midstream: The Story of a Mother's Death and a Daughter's Renewal*. New York: Viking Penguin, 1991.

Selye, Hans. *Stress without Distress*. New York: NAL–Dutton, 1975.

Shames, Laurence. *The Hunger for More: Searching for Values in an Age of Greed*. New York: Random, 1989.

Sheehy, Gail. *Pathfinders: Overcoming the Crises of Adult Life and Finding Your Own Path to Well-Being*. New York: Bantam, 1981.

Siegel, Bernie. *Love, Medicine and Miracles: Lessons Learned about Self-Healing from a Surgeon's Experience with Exceptional Patients*. New York: Harper and Row, 1986.

Tavris, Carol. *Anger: The Misunderstood Emotion.* New York: Simon and Schuster, 1989.

Terkel, Studs. *Working.* New York: Ballantine, 1985.

Toffler, Alvin. *Powershift: Knowledge, Wealth, and Violence at the Edge of the 21st Century.* New York: Bantam, 1990.

Voltaire. *Candide, Zadig and Selected Poems.* Translated by Donald M. Frame. Bloomington, IN: University of Indiana Press, 1961.

Wallerstein, Judith. *Second Chances.* New York: Ticknor and Fields, 1989.

Whitman, Walt. *Leaves of Grass.* New York: Doubleday, 1940.

Wurman, Richard Saul. *Information Anxiety.* New York: Doubleday, 1989.

Yankelovich, Daniel. *New Rules: Searching for Self-Fulfillment in a World Turned Upside Down.* New York: Random, 1981.

York, Phyllis and David York. *Tough Love: A Self-Help Manual for Parents Troubled by Teenage Behavior.* Sellersville, PA: Community Service Foundation, 1980.

Resources - Complementary

Bodner, Joanne and Venda Raye-Johnson. *Staying Up When Your Job Pulls You Down*. New York: Perigee Books, 1991.

Bolles, Richard. *What Color Is Your Parachute?* Berkeley, CA: Ten Speed Press, 1991.

Chilton, David. *The Wealthy Barber: The Common Sense Guide to Successful Financial Planning*. Toronto: Stoddart, 1989.

Cooper, Robert K. *Health & Fitness Excellence: The Scientific Action Plan*. Boston: Houghton Mifflin, 1989.

Cousins, Norman. *Head First: The Biology of Hope*. New York: Dutton, 1989.

Covey, Stephen R. *The Seven Habits of Highly Effective People: Restoring the Character Ethic*. New York: Simon and Schuster, 1989.

Dubin, Judith and Melanie Keveles. *Fired for Success: How to Turn Losing a Job into the Opportunity of a Lifetime!* New York: Warner, 1990.

Dyer, Wayne. *What Do You Really Want for Your Children?* New York: Avon, 1985.

Hanson, Peter G. *Stress for Success: Thriving On Stress At Work*. Toronto: Collins, 1989.

Jaffe, Dennis and Cynthia Scott. *Take This Job and Love It: How to Change Your Work without Changing Your Job*. New York: Simon and Schuster, 1988.

Kanchier, Carole. *Questers: Dare to Change Your Job and Your Life*. Toronto: Key Porter, 1988.

Lederer, William J. *Mirages of Marriage*. New York: Norton, 1990.

Maccoby, Michael. *Why Work? Motivating and Leading the New Generation*. New York: Touchstone, 1988.

McMakin, Jacqueline. *Working from the Heart: For Those Who Hunger for Meaning and Satisfaction in Their Work*. San Diego: Luramedia, 1989.

Merrill, Douglas and Donna Douglas. *Manage Your Time, Manage Your Work, Manage Yourself*. New York: AMACOM, 1980.

Morgan, Hal and Kerry Tucker. *Companies that Care: The Most Family-Friendly Companies in America — What They Offer, and How They Got That Way*. New York: Simon and Schuster, 1991.

Olds, Sally Wendkos. *The Working Parents Survival Guide*. Rocklin, CA: Prima Publishing and Communication, 1989.

Ruben, Harvey L. *Supermarriage: Overcoming the Predictable Crises of Married Life*. New York: Bantam, 1986.

Sinetar, Marsha. *Do What You Love, the Money will Follow: Discovering the Right Livelihood*. New York: Dell, 1989.

Wylie, Betty Jane. *All in the Family: A Survival Guide for Family Living and Loving in a Changing World*. Toronto: Key Porter, 1988.